God's Lively People

Books by Mark Gibbs and T. Ralph Morton
Published by The Westminster Press

God's Lively People
God's Frozen People

God's Lively People

God's Lively People

by Mark Gibbs and T. Ralph Morton

The Westminster Press/Philadelphia

ISBN 0–664–24914–0

Library of Congress Catalog Card No. 77–142997

Published by The Westminster Press ®
Philadelphia, Pennsylvania

PRINTED IN THE UNITED STATES OF AMERICA

Contents

Introduction

God's *Lively* People? The title of our first book on the laity, *God's Frozen People*, was considered by some people more than a trifle depressing; this time we shall perhaps be criticized for an unfashionable optimism. Yet we are absolutely convinced that, despite all the difficulties of our times and all the gloom and fearfulness of so many church writers, there are still many—and there could be many more—potentially strong, determined, concerned and lively Christian laymen. They can learn to face both the strains of today and the uncertainties and possibilities of tomorrow.

At the moment many of these men and women are anxiously and awkwardly critical of the institutional churches. They are impatient for intelligent and efficient church organization and leadership; and they have almost given up hope that church education—from the sermon to the confirmation class—can prove relevant to their situation in the modern world. It is urgently necessary that the good and harrassed leaders of our churches take this whole matter of laity education much more seriously. For the plain fact for such church bureaucrats is: today you can no longer have a docile laity, a submissive flock of 'good, faithful people' who will obey what senior clergy order or request. There are only two alternatives. Either we shall have an increasingly unresponsive and unco-operative laity, often not understanding what the clergy want, unwilling to join in their grand plans, giving less and less financially, and often taking no part or even interest in the paper synods and conferences of the various denominations.

Or, if our church leaders will take the risk and invest a considerable proportion of their dwindling revenues in laity education, then there is, we believe, still a good chance of producing, not a submissive, but an educated, alert, critical and lively laity. They will still give the church leadership a bad time, for they will insist on serving God in his world rather than tamely following outdated ecclesiastical traditions. But they will be *alive*, and there is more than a slender chance that in the generous freedom of the Holy Spirit they will—no doubt painfully and ruthlessly—renew the structures of the churches in their scanty spare time.

Such are the alternatives before church leaders in Britain and in the world today. We suggest, with respect, that they have dodged this issue for too long, and that they now have very little time left in which to choose. Already, thousands of the best laity have given up hope in the institutional churches. There are now not so very many left—especially in countries like Britain and Australia, and especially under the age of fifty. How much longer must we wait before our church leaders— and treasurers—learn to make a major investment *in people and in the future?*

We are most grateful for comments and criticisms given us in the heavy work of preparing this book. It simply is not possible to mention everyone, but we are particularly indebted to The Rev. Canon David L. Edwards, The Rev. Murray Leishman, The Rev. Douglas Galbraith and The Rev. David Millar for their help. We should like, also, to take this opportunity to express our gratitude to our colleagues on the Board of Trustees and the U.S. Committee of the Audenshaw Foundation: in Britain Mrs Basil Higginson, The Rev. Francis House, The Rev. W. H. Wright and The Rev. Trevor Beeson, and in the United States Mr John Tillson, Mr Tom Matheny, Mrs T. O. Wedel, Mrs Vernon Newbold, Professor Franklin H. Littell, Dr C. Arild Olsen, and Dr William H. Schechter. Their constant and perceptive concern for the cause of laity education is a great encouragement to us. None of these people, of course, should be held liable for the opinions in and the failings of this book.

We also wish to thank very sincerely Mrs J. Jardine, Mrs C. Morton, Mrs F. Platt and Mrs S. Figures for their fine secretarial assistance. We have been most fortunate in this.

Some parts of this book have appeared in draft form in issues of *Christian Comment* and the *Audenshaw Papers*, and appear here by courtesy of the Audenshaw Foundation.

We should add in explanation that this United States edition of *God's Lively People* differs in some respects from the British edition published by Messrs Collins in London. Chapter 7, 'What Has Gone Wrong?' has been specially written to replace Chapters 7 and 8 in the British edition. Chapter 14, 'The Way Forward,' and the Bibliography have also undergone extensive revision. We have made these alterations not only because the situation of the laity in the United States is in some ways very different from that in Britain and in Europe but also because we are convinced that members of the great American churches still possess an important and special potential for the future. If they can learn to transfer their secular Monday-through-Friday genius for innovation in scientific and industrial affairs into their church and political involvements, then they may yet find renewal for their churches and their country, and give new strengths to the life of the whole world-wide Church.

M.G.

T.R.M.

Part One
A Faith for Tomorrow's World

1. A Commitment to the Future

This book has not been written out of any sense of despair or defeat. We believe that God has given his people many signs of hope for the future, many new ways of service, and many new styles of learning together. The present wave of self-criticism among the churches may be uncomfortable and abrasive, but it is infinitely better than a smug complacency. It can bring genuine renewal if Christian leaders learn to use it constructively and intelligently.

Nevertheless, the outlook for many churches, at least in Western countries, seems confused and unpromising at the moment. Both in Britain and in the United States the economic and political scenes are uncertain. Bitter controversies over racism, poverty and student rights are questioning and sometimes threatening to destroy—very rapidly—hopes of human co-operation and community built up over many weary years. Problems of world hunger and political oppression—reported so urgently each night from almost every corner of the globe—crowd in upon our private and local lives, and mock our tiny resources for compassion or sensitivity. The great church structures of our day—ecumenical, Catholic, or Protestant—plod conscientiously on, often through a barrage of angry criticism from ecclesiastical 'drop outs'; but they seem incapable of producing or recruiting leaders who will capture the interest of the laity or even show that they understand them.

In these circumstances, it is impossible for us to discuss the education of Christian lay people without first admitting some of the major pressures on them today, whether they be top decision-makers or ordinary workers

and housewives. On an American television programme
the distinguished industrialist J. Irwin Miller was heard
to say 'I'm a business man. I spend my time choosing between two wrongs, and being shot down for the one I
choose.' That was a realistic admission from a prominent
Christian layman; and the same can be said for many
people involved in politics, business, trade unions and
the like—and especially if they are not at the top of the
ladder. Most of them want to do 'the decent thing'; but it
is not easy to distinguish this in the confusing swirl of
ethical 'greys' in life, between which they have to decide
—and quickly, before the board meeting or the union
ballot tomorrow morning. Life is not the simple good-
versus-bad morality of the Sunday-school lessons, nor is
it the leisured ethical debate of traditional theological
education. It is messy, confused, and urgent; and there is
never enough money to go round, at least for anyone
concerned with education or social work. Laity education must be concerned with such hard realities of public
and private lives today, and with the responsible compromises by which men live and run the world (and
which are infinitely preferable to the irresponsible, un-
thinking compromises into which we may all so easily
slide).

God's Lively People is written in the conviction that
this is the stuff of the Christian life today and for the
future, as it always has been; and that about the one
absolute that the Church can demand of a man is a total
commitment to live in this kind of world, and not to run
away from it. We have a commitment to get involved,
to relate the faith to the uncertainties and agonies of the
twentieth and twenty-first centuries, and not to retreat
psychologically to the nineteenth. To be involved does
not mean that we must lose ourselves simplistically or
romantically in the fads or the enthusiasms of the moment. It is to take St Matthew Chapter 25 seriously, to
realize that 'inasmuch' as we do not help the poor, the

lonely and the sick intelligently and efficiently in our modern complicated economy we do not meet and know God himself today. It is to realize that if there is sin and vice in the world of the modern city, there may also be the sins and vices of spiritual selfishness in the worship and clubs of suburban churches. And to be involved is to understand what it means to live in a modern democracy and not in a mediaeval village or a slave state.

Many church people in recent years have come to understand the present weakness of the institutional Church; and have become thoroughly disillusioned and depressed about the whole business. Often they are in some danger of becoming 'Christian anarchists', prepared to destroy and to desert old structures without offering new models to take their place. Others seem to be asking for some kind of Christian 'magic' to renew the Church. They almost rejoice in catastrophes and human miseries, suggesting that by these we are to be disciplined by the Lord and brought back to loyal dutiful nineteenth-century church behaviours. Others have become apathetic about church renewal. 'When the Lord will, he will send blessing', as if God were entirely capricious about the spiritual goodies he bestows.

Such theories about church renewal are an insult to God and to his creation. Men are not meant to be puppets dancing to the storms or balmy breezes of heaven, nor frightened slaves cowering before their lord's punishments. We are called to a mature manhood in partnership with him, to a discipline certainly, but a *discipline of discovery, of reform and of renewal*. The way forward is not to take refuge in magical or superstitious theories of heavenly blessings, but to have an intelligent commitment to the future, in which we join the whole of mankind in its quest for an orderly and humane style of life. This will give us from time to time a severe pain in the mind; but it will be worth it.

The discipline of discovery is familiar enough to scientists, technologists, and many of those who run our modern world. It is indeed the way by which over the last two hundred years 'man has come of age', to use the often misunderstood phrase of Dietrich Bonhoeffer. It does not, of course, imply that mankind has become a truly mature race, a perfect race, a sinless or a wholly sensible race. It simply means that we are different from previous generations. We have 'the key to the door', we are about the age of twenty-one—or at least eighteen. We are no longer children crying in the dark or shivering in the cold: we know how to fix the lights and turn on the heating. We have tremendous problems—and we assess them much more carefully than in the past (that in itself makes us different and gives us a chance to lick them). We are painfully aware of the deep questions of poverty and wickedness which haunt this planet. And we are determined to find some answers. As a race, we know more of our strengths and weaknesses than ever before.

This discipline of discovery can, of course, be used for tremendous good or for appalling evil. It may offer us a new foodstuff for India's millions, or a new nerve gas for mass annihilation. Within the Church, too, it can be used for wicked purposes; for everything in the Church, as outside it, can be sanctified or corrupted. But unless we all understand something of the intellectual processes involved, we cannot even see whether our country and our Church are corrupted or not.

The first element in this discipline of discovery is to be prepared to look calmly and carefully at the future. To consider the twenty-first century more important than the nineteenth. To understand the pace of change in the world today, and where it is probably leading us. C. P. Snow in his book *The Two Cultures* makes some sharp, and somewhat exaggerated, distinctions between scientifically oriented people on the one hand, and literary and artistic types on the other. The difference, he says, is that the scientists 'have the future in their bones'.

Lord Snow should not be allowed to reserve such privileges for the scientists. All Christians must, by their theology and their understanding of creation, have the future—as well as the past—in their bones. And they must understand the scientific revolution in human thought—mostly brought about by the scientists and social scientists—which produces this attitude of mind and of spirit.

Many of our readers will know something of the different attempts now made to study the future, in the United States, in the Netherlands, in Britain, and elsewhere. A convenient interim report of the work of such specialists in the United States can be found in the book, *The Year 2000*, by H. Kahn and A. J. Wiener (see Bibliography). It is already a highly exciting intellectual study, particularly since the team of scholars involved have no illusions that the year 2000 will automatically show some kind of 'progress' on today. Hopefully it will, but nothing is certain; and the book offers alternative 'scenarios' suggesting optimistic, pessimistic, and 'surprise-free' projections for the next thirty years.

The depressing thing is that even in the United States the churches have so far shown little expertise in such intellectual speculation about the future.[1] The Commission on the Year 2000 reports rather ruefully (in *Daedalus*, issue of October 1968) that they feel that the ethical and moral implications of their study have been thin and largely unexplored. They certainly do not seem to wish to rule out such investigations; and where (as in the Netherlands) a group of Protestant and Roman Catholic

1. It is possible that some of the major US churches may join in the new Institute for the Future, but they are not yet committed to this.

theologians have attempted to make contact with the Dutch *Workgroep 2000* they have been welcomed. But the whole idea of being future-oriented in this way is so difficult for many church leaders and church scholars. In every theological college of any repute there is—very properly—at least one professor of Christian history. But where are our professors of Christian future?

The modern Christian must not only think hard about the future, he must also plan and prepare for it in the normal way of secular innovators. Such a technique is familiar enough to those of our readers who are scientists or engineers or businessmen. It involves a process of:

Research . . . Development . . . Information

Research

Basic research is one of the most important human activities, and there is a considerable literature on its support and organization. We cannot enter here into the important arguments about individual research versus planned, group research, about the eccentricities of pure scientists and thinkers, and the problems of finding, hiring, and freeing very able men and women so that they can do their best work. There are only a few rules in the game, and these are comparatively simple. *First:* you must identify promising people early in their working lives. So many genuinely new ideas have come to us in the twentieth century from men under thirty years of age. *Second:* you must deliver such people from routine administration, from trivial scientific and engineering work, and from at least the most serious financial worries of themselves and their families. And *third:* you must let them say the wildest things, dream up the most impossible organizations, and try, before they are too old, to see visions. For if they come up with ideas which are immediately acceptable to ordinary dull mortals, they are probably not doing basic research at all.

In as much as the Church ever encourages any basic research, it breaks almost all these rules almost all the time. Time off for thinking is a basic necessity for first-class employees, and Shell or Unilever will recognize this (and not only for their scientists). Such research grants as there are in the churches[2] are normally granted to distinctly senior scholars, and are sometimes a reward for past faithfulness rather than an incentive to innovation. We have, still, a considerable number of bright young lay people and clergy in the churches, but if they are not suppressed and discouraged anyway as dangerous radicals, they are swamped by speaking engagements and church committees, and blackmailed to be 'loyal' enough to undertake every trivial task that comes along.

Development

The institutional Church is even worse in understanding and in providing for development work. In the secular world, this is recognized as often the most infuriating and difficult and expensive period of all. It is not easy to take a basic new idea such as the laser, and to turn it into a reliable, safe, cheap, and saleable product. To take an idea such as career guidance, and to turn it into a practicable organization that local teachers and parents and employers can use. To get the bugs out of a new product, or to iron out the difficulties in a new style of community organization, or a new tax system. This kind of thing requires time and patience. It requires a suitable modesty until the snags are dealt with. It requires the risking of a good deal of money and staff time.

2. They are mostly tied to the past. You can get money for research into the history of the laity in the thirteenth century, but very little for planning ahead into the future.

There was once, we understand, a firm which thought of marketing a new kind of washing machine. This was to work by ultrasonic rays, which would attack the molecules of dirt in the clothes and remove them from the fabric. (We believe that the idea is theoretically practicable.) Unfortunately the development job took rather a long time. The story is that occasionally, when the machine was started, there was a very alarming grating sound and after a few minutes both clothes and tub disintegrated into a nasty mess of steel, brass, and textiles on the laboratory floor. The rays were rather too strong. Rather more often, the tub remained intact but, when after a few minutes the lid was lifted, the clothes were found in an unattractive mess of rags and buttons at the bottom of the machine. This, too, was hardly a strong selling point for the new product. But most of the time, indeed ninety-nine per cent of the time, whether you lifted the lid after five minutes, five hours, or five days made no difference. The clothes just stayed dirty.[3]

Such unfortunate snags in the development of a new product or system are common enough; but the institutional Church seems scarcely to recognize this. There is hardly ever an adequate allocation of staff and of money for a new experiment in, say, university ministries, or industrial missions, or house churches (all ideas which in the last twenty years have run into considerable development snags).

Information

Information about new theories and products is unbelievably swift these days. News of the laser was apparently on television and in the weekly magazines so quickly

3. We are now promised for the 1970s ultrasonic washing machines which will work satisfactorily.

that many school science teachers were embarrassed by this and by the questions of their pupils. If one were to devise, say in Edinburgh, something as trivial as a new supermarket cart (perhaps one which would play cheerful tunes as it was loaded by the suburban housewife) then news about it would flow like lightning around the commercial world. Within a few days, eager executives would jet in from London, New York, Toronto, San Francisco, from Rotterdam and Frankfurt, from Tokyo and from Sydney. There is an international community —if not of scholarship, of inventiveness—among world salesmen. This is much more true among world physicists, economists, doctors, and so on.

But not in the Church. Ideas flow round the world Church with the speed of cold tar. We live, still, in the age of the Spanish galleon and the covered wagon. It is extremely depressing to find that in so many great cities the ordinary members of church A have not the slightest idea what church B—20 miles away—is experimenting with, still less what church C—500 miles away and in another denomination and country—has been up to. Here is surely one of the greatest weaknesses of the ecumenical movement. We are truly a world Church, not when occasionally Catholic bishops and Baptist superintendents sip coffee together, but when we learn what the rest of the Church is doing, when we learn from each other, when we get moving in experimentation together. If a Roman Catholic meets a Methodist for the first time, or an Anglican talks with a Congregationalist, the first serious questions he ought to ask are: 'Now, what has God told you lately? What have you found out that we don't know yet?'

One can gauge the lack of communication between the churches on questions of the education of the laity by one simple fact. At the date of writing, there are some fifty theological college libraries in Britain, and some three hundred in the United States. Yet, so far as we can check, in not one of them is there an adequate working file of reports from the major experiments in laity education which have been undertaken since 1945, and which are now under way. We do not speak of a scholarly and complete collection but of a simple set of books and other documents which would help experimenters and students at least to find where they ought to look next, and to learn which innovators are likely to answer some of their first questions.

If the first task of a communications network is to let fellow workers know what is happening, what has been achieved and what has failed, then the second and major task is to let the ordinary people—the man in the street —know as soon as some workable new model has been produced and is available. Of course developments both in commercial advertising and in popular education have broken down many barriers here. With all its defects, the modern advertising industry certainly lets everybody know pretty quickly when a new product or service is available; and the television, the popular magazines, and the wonderful deluge of paperbacks help our exploding school and university education systems to add new ideas and information to formal classroom teaching. It does not take long for a young man, even in central Africa, to learn about the VC10 or the miniskirt. Indeed, we all now know that it is only by continually learning, constantly hearing about new ideas and products, and constantly retraining and re-educating ourselves that we can survive in the modern world, where the pace of change is such that at least one hundred years of our grandparents' world are crammed into twenty-five of ours, so that a man of seventy-five is now something like three hundred years old. The amazing thing is that while some old—and middle-aged—people find the strain severe, so many men and women are wonderfully flexible and adaptable to new ideas. The present grandmothers in Moscow or Liverpool, and the farmers in India or Kansas, are making a fine job of understanding products and techniques unknown ten years ago. They have to; for otherwise they cannot survive.

This is very obvious in many professional and business occupations. The *Wall Street Journal* has carried some sad tales of business executives who, having gained a top job, achieved their second car, and their magnificent mortgage, find already at forty or forty-five (not at fifty-five or sixty-five) that they are being elbowed out by bright young graduates of twenty-five or thirty, with inconvenient new skills in data processing or drug technology or overseas marketing. In many more ordinary jobs, too, you must go on learning constantly, or you are finished. Very many workers are already using machines in industry or distribution which had not been heard of when they finished school. Almost everyone may have to be retrained for a new job once or twice in one working lifetime.

It is the same in much of our social and public life. The housewife has to learn new skills in buying and using new products—and in spotting the new cunning with which manufacturers may try to exploit her innocence. It is desperately necessary that citizens update their political loyalties and beliefs, so that a British election is not fought with the old slogans of the 1930s, and a United States senator can ask his home state to consider the new foreign policies his country requires so urgently in the '70s. The position here is not as black as many prophets have foretold. In particular, the informal education in public affairs offered by many television programmes is often extremely effective in giving ordinary people a chance to hear new ideas, which perhaps their local papers and their local gossip have ignored or ignorantly sneered at. The great emphasis now on adult education all over the world is a sign that, not only in their working lives but also as citizens and human beings, men and women are eager to have the chance to learn new things and to argue about new ideas. Indeed people can be divided into two groups, regardless of age. Those who have acquired the habit of *continually learning*, continually asking questions, continually facing new ideas (without accepting every new fad and fashion uncritically). And those who at fifteen, or twenty-five (a dangerous age), or fifty-five, have slipped into the attitude that they now know enough, and whose minds have gradually shut fast, and whose only psychological refuge will be a wistful remembering of 'the good old days'. They are intellectual cabbages.

It is no different in the Church. Of course the Gospel is not a 'product' to be sold, nor a piece of educational machinery to be updated. But if we believe that God calls us to be faithful in our time and generation, then we have to reckon with that time and generation—which is one in which the price of survival is to be *constantly learning*. Certainly often in informal ways and not in formal schools or colleges, but learning all the days until we die. Yet very many church leaders are still content to think of education—and therefore Christian education—as something almost entirely for children. In the future, Christian education both for the young and for adults must be planned as a continuous process, starting, certainly, in early childhood, but *increasing* in its impact in student and early adult years (instead of dwindling away then) and carrying on through the years of early married life, through middle age, and up to the years of senior citizenship. It is tragic that Christian education in so many churches stops just at the age when in secular education boys and girls move on to exciting, new, adult knowledge: when their biology lessons—or the TV documentary—give them the chance to argue about the Pill or about abortion; when they begin to understand from lessons or student arguments or a paperback what modern war is really like. There are so many graduates in our modern world—and this applies to Kampala and Delhi as much as to Edinburgh or Harvard—who have an adult knowledge of secular problems, but only a kid's knowledge of the faith, and who have never been encouraged to relate the two at all. As Jacob Nussbaumer wrote in *Audenshaw Papers*, No. 2 (describing the state of religious education in Switzerland): 'One thing we have not done. We have never tried to see the world with the eyes of the Bible, and the Bible with the eyes of the world. The result has often been a kind of faith which is not able to stand reality.'

The churches still have too many ministers, too many Sunday-school leaders and too many parents who themselves have never thought through the development of children in this way, who do not quite understand what the process of education today is like and how adolescents can make the most of it, and who certainly do not see what can be done about the tremendous leakage of young people from any kind of religious church life—whether it be Anglican or Baptist—as soon as they begin to grow up.

It is in this sense that this book is about Christian education. 'Christian Education' is not an appealing phrase to many people. To many British readers it may conjure up memories of rather childish Sunday-school classes, or reading through unattractive bits of the Old Testament in dull day-school periods. Even to American readers, the words 'Christian Ed.' mean essentially something for younger children, something that stops at confirmation, or at fifteen, or at least as soon as you can consider yourself grown-up. Sometimes people prefer to talk about 'lay training' or 'youth training'; but this, too, has unfortunate overtones—as if the laity are to be trained to perform tricks while the parson offers them a judicious mixture of religious sticks and carrots. The French are lucky: they use the term *formation laïque*, and the Germans have an equivalent, *Laienbildung*; but one can hardly talk in English about Laity Formation—

as if Christians were to be moulded like jellies. So we are bold to suggest that the right phrase for what we are after is 'Christian Education', in the widest and deepest and broadest sense of those words.

After all, it is recognized today in the secular world that education means much more than instruction and drilling in formal knowledge. Most people understand that it means the whole learning process, by which people come to new knowledge and experience. And it is accepted that education is more than school classes and college lectures: it involves a great deal of discussion and dialogue and argument. More than this, any first-class education process faces you with a challenge to make decisions to accept or reject new ideas as they come to you. It means more than expert A giving knowledge to student B: it often involves an argument in which student B offers ideas to expert A, and *in which both teacher and student learn together*. And—above all —it is now clear that education for modern man can never stop. It must be a continuous process, reaching far beyond school leaving age, continuing in formal and informal ways, in lectures and in short work courses, in TV programmes and in arguments in the pub, until we die. For since the world is now in a state of constant change, the wisdom we have inherited from our fathers and grandfathers is only part of what we need if we are to adapt to the world of tomorrow.

We venture to take for granted in *God's Lively People* certain of our main themes in *God's Frozen People*. We assume that the Church is not essentially buildings, nor a denomination, nor just the clergy and ministers and full-time church workers. The Church is the whole People of God together, all the men and women and children called to be Christians, whether they are ordained or confirmed or not. Whether they are archbishops or architects or advertising agents, whether they are ministers or mothers or miners, whether they are deacons or divers or dentists. And whether they left full-time education at fifteen or at twenty-five; and whether they are Roman Catholic or Presbyterian or Salvation Army. The Church of Christ is still hideously divided, and the vast majority of its members—the laity—still leave far too much to the tiny proportion of Christians who are full-time paid clergy; but people are now beginning to realize what a Church might be like in which a good proportion of the laity both took their responsibilities seriously and also fully recognized their fellow Christians in other denominations and in other callings.

We take all this for granted. And we also assume that such attitudes ought to be encouraged from the first in young people, rather than offered later at some conference or other as a corrective to wrong ideas about the Church and the laity, which have been learnt at school or Sunday school or from parents. We are not at all convinced that the training of the laity is something that has to happen *despite* the usual pattern of school and parish education : we are sure that it ought to be something offered to lively young people in and through their normal upbringing.

Like *God's Frozen People* this is meant to be a practical little book. Whole libraries of far more learned and detailed works have been written on many of the subjects we discuss; and if in our first book we seemed to say little new to some of the professional theologians who write about the laity, it is certain that in this one we shall seem to say little to the more advanced experts in the methods of adult Christian education. Some details of their work can be found in our Bibliography. We are well content with the way in which *God's Frozen People* has been received by ordinary educated people— whether they are to be found in the church pew on Sunday or not. We simply tried to bridge the gap (which is much wider than many people think) between the experts on the laity and the laymen themselves. We have similar modest ambitions for *God's Lively People* : we hope that our approach may be found useful to those who still believe that God's people may be kept high-spirited and sharp and critical, as well as dedicated and active and prayerful. There is a third way between the tragic dilemma which seems to face so many men and women as they come of age. They need neither give up the Church as irrelevant to their modern lives, nor lose their liveliness as they grow older in the faith.

2. What the Secular World Is Like

Men today live in a new world. This is a platitude and, like many platitudes, our way of dodging the implications of a terrifying fact. We have to recognize that the world now is different, and in what ways it is different from the world of last century. It is easy to point to the things that are new : nuclear power, the aeroplane, space travel, television, race riots, students' demonstrations, the clash between world poverty and Western affluence. But does not the difference really go much deeper? Has there not been a fundamental change in our attitude to the world, to its recognition of itself?

The word 'secular' is often applied to our modern world, generally in condemnation. Many people use it to indicate that something has gone wrong with the world, that it sees no need for religion or the idea of God, that it is self-sufficient and concerned solely with its own ends. This is not the sense in which the word 'secular' is used in this book. We use it to describe a world that has cut itself free from many of its old superstitions and fears and that, both in terror and in hope, knows that its destiny is in its own hands. We use it also because it recalls us to the truth, which is asserted in the Bible from beginning to end, *that it is only in this world that we can know God and that it is only in the contemporary world that we can serve him*. This may not be the meaning that is usually given to the word. But we shall all need to put this fuller meaning into the word if we are to see our Christian duty in the world today. And, indeed, the word 'secular' has taken on different meanings in its history. Basically it means temporal, belonging to time. It's the word that for hundreds of years has been used in the worship of the Roman Catholic Church to express the idea of 'for ever and ever'—*in saecula saeculorum*. Its later, more specific use is to claim the world of space and time for God, as in describing a parish priest as 'secular' in distinction from a monk who was 'religious'. In the last century a new word, 'secularism', was introduced, to express the idea that man was self-sufficient and had no need of the hypothesis of God. It is this meaning that is now often attached to the word 'secular'. It is in protest against this that we have to recover the true use of the word, to assert the belief that time, as well as space, is God's creation and where we know him. A. T. van Leeuwen, the Dutch theologian, can write : 'secularization may be broadly described as the creative and liberating activity of the Word of God'.[1] Perhaps such a provocative use of the word will help us to think. It is with this purpose that the word is used here.

But, because the word 'religious' still has a meaning for us, Christians sometimes talk as if there were two worlds opposed to each other, and they lived in them both and could choose which to serve. Indeed, they often talk as if there were a lot of worlds to which they belonged and they could jump from one to the other—the political world, the academic world, the world of sport, the world of the Church. But the word 'secular' will tolerate no such division, any more than the word 'Christian' will. Men know only one world, as they know only one life. We can give it whatever name we like but we cannot divide it. When we think of the activities in which we are engaged, in industry and commerce, in service and in politics, we can justify them in terms of their usefulness to men or in terms of the glory of God. And the more we think about it the more surprised we'll be to find the terms coincide. What we cannot do is to sort them out into two classes. What we are talking about is the ordinary world of our daily lives: the world we live in, the world we work in, the world that serves us and that we serve, the world that terrifies us, the world that we enjoy. For us there isn't any other world. If there were a better word to describe it than the word 'secular' we'd use it. But if there isn't, let's call it secular.

The most important task for us is to try to recognize the features of this new world of ours. It doesn't matter whether it is with relief or regret that we see that the world has changed. It does matter that we should know how it has changed. If our discussion of how we should live in the world today and how we should educate ourselves for this life is to be of any use, then we should *know* something about the world in which we live. We can't take this knowledge for granted any more than we can take our understanding of the Christian faith for granted—or our knowledge of ourselves.

It would be hopeless to try to enumerate all the changes that have taken place and are taking place in the world today. All that we can do is to point out four of the main features of the map of this new world. These would not have been evident, except in hints of what was to come, before 1914.

The first has been mentioned, but something more must be said about it. For the first time in the world's history we can talk about the world as *one*. Before this century men did not think of the world as a unity. They thought of it as divided by time and space into a number of worlds: 'the Roman World', 'the Ancient World', 'the Christian World', 'the World of Islam', 'the New World'. The world for men was the world they knew, the world they lived in. If they thought of those who lived elsewhere, they thought of them as living in a different world, as if the earth were made up of many distinct and

separate worlds, with buffers of empty space or unknown history between. And because of this, men before
us have been impressed by the vastness of the earth, by
its unexplored and empty spaces.

Today we begin to see the earth as almost too small
for us. Two things emphasize this. One is that we can
travel round the earth in a few hours and can take
photographs of it from outer space. We see it as men
have never seen it before, as a very small object in space.
The other is our realization that the earth is getting too
small for its inhabitants. There is now no space for them
to live at peace. Soon, by reason of an exploding population, there may be no room to live at all. There is now
no undiscovered part of the world to absorb the excesses
of the world we know. It's one world now. We've got to
live on it. This is implied in the use of the word 'secular'.
It emphasizes that it is this small, known unit that we
are speaking about. It's a new picture of the world.

Then, because it is a unity and the barriers between
the former little worlds are down, it's for the first time
an *open* world. We now live in this world with other
people. Of course men have always known that there
were other people in the world, but they have generally
managed to keep them at a distance. Now we know that
we share the world with other men. We can no longer
escape from them. We don't like this. We resent it. We
fight against it. We can't get away from the conviction
that the only proper society is the closed society. We
still think of the village as the ideal place for men to live
because there every one knows every one else and knows
their background; and because each inhabitant of the village has his recognized place, the stranger is looked
upon with suspicion. The happy family was the self-contained family which kept itself to itself, and its symbol
was the door locked on the inside.

This exclusiveness was also the national ideal. The aim
of the nation was self-preservation by defence or by

conquest. The frontier was where you defied the foreigner. China built its wall to keep the barbarians out. Britain was glad to be an island. Christendom saw itself as a citadel on the defensive against infidels and pagans. It developed the characteristics of a besieged society—the rigid authority of military and ecclesiastical law, the discipline that demanded obedience from every subject, the excitement of occasional bloody forays of revenge or conquest as in the Crusades. Christendom has implanted in our minds the picture of the Christian as a soldier fighting against great odds. We see it expressed in many of our hymns. We see it in our inability to get on with people. We see it in the feeling of safety which many Christians seem to have only when they are in violent opposition.

But Christendom was destroyed long ago. The barriers that cut us off from other people are down. During the last three hundred years they have been broken down by men's curiosity about the rest of the world and about other men. They have been broken down by exploration and trade and by the Church's foreign missionary enterprise, which jumped over the lines that the theologians had drawn. And finally they were laid flat by the unity of science, and the realization that men are the same all over the world.

We don't like it. We feel bewildered in this new world. We regret the old self-contained life. We try to get back to it on holiday—to the place we knew as children when we did not think of the world outside, or to a foreign country where life seems, because of its strangeness, more self-contained than it really is. But we know that we can't keep ourselves to ourselves any longer. The key that locked the door is lost, or it's in the hands of those who are outside, who now can come in when they want. We are inextricably involved with other people: with people we know and people we don't know; with people we see and people we don't see; with people we like and people we don't like. We know that we need them if we are to live our new kind of life. We need men and women from overseas to run our buses and to staff our hospitals. We need the raw materials that men in other lands produce. We need them to buy our goods if our national trade budget is to balance. We need the goods and services of other nations and we like to think that they need ours. This involvement with the peoples of the world is evident in our shops, in the board-rooms of industry and in parliament. Economically we share our life with all other people and are dependent on them, even if in our private lives we try to pretend that we can shut the door and lock it.

We find this open world very uncomfortable. We try to escape. Some of us escape by becoming absorbed in ourselves; in our career, in some special interest, in religion, in mysticism. Some of us escape by identifying ourselves with some authority that makes a particular and absolute demand, whether it be a political party or a church. But we can't escape from the open secular world. We can't escape from it and we can't dominate it. We can't bring men to unity by conquest or destruction or conversion. No section of the world—Christian or communist, Chinese or American—will ever be able to enforce its will on the world. In an open world we have to learn to live together—Christians and communists, Moslems and Buddhists, East and West. And probably we have the chance to do it only if we refuse to accept the deepest division of all—into rich and poor. This is the only division now that really matters—the only division that could destroy the world.

This is the new open world in which we live. It is very strange to us. It demands the cultivation and exercise of virtues we have extolled but rarely practised—toleration, humility and love—in place of the qualities we have practised and almost come to praise—pride, intolerance and persecution.

The third feature of our modern, secular world may seem superficial in comparison. It is the *uniform* way of life that is being created throughout the world. We call it by different names. We talk about industrialization and urbanization, about the new metropolis and the secular society. Generally we use these terms in a superior, critical sense. We still look at life from the standpoint of the isolated, rural community. We think of this new way of life as soulless, and also as existing everywhere but where we happen to live. Our place of residence is somehow always a bit different, because we are familiar with it and, indeed, enjoy living in it.

This new uniformity is a way of life rather than a collection of places. It's the way of life of all who are engaged in industry and commerce, in service, education and administration, and it is becoming more and more the same in style throughout the world. Despite differences in aims and theories, the organization of industry becomes increasingly similar in the USA and in the USSR. The large unit of production and the new technocratic manager become the pattern everywhere. Of course as yet the majority of the inhabitants of the world do not share this life. It means little to the starving peasants of Brazil. But the future of their children depends on their being brought into this life, and their present poverty cannot stop the spread of this way of life, which will become more and more determinitive of the future of men on the earth. It may be that China will evolve a pattern of life different from the patterns we already know in East and West. But it will still be a pattern based on modern scientific techniques, however used.

We may be tempted to say that this uniform, urban, industrial way of life is superficial and spread very thin; that it is manifest in the new towns and rebuilt cities that we create, but affects very little the life of the ordinary people who live in them and not at all those—the great majority of the world—who do not. But it is becoming a pretty massive uniformity. It is indeed superficial in that it is obvious. Airports throughout the world are almost of the same design and of the same appearance. The traveller is glad that the name is usually indicated in large letters, for otherwise he might be uncertain where he was. The commercial cities of the world grow more and more alike. Brussels and Baltimore look very much the same, with their flyovers and tunnels, with the same cars in the streets and the same advertisements on the posters. Supermarkets, stores and shops and the things they sell are much the same wherever you go. Means of production, methods of buying and selling, means of transport are the same everywhere. And this is also true of sport, amusement, and art. People in different countries can watch the same football match or listen to the same pop concert at the same time. We can begin to talk about a common culture which is based on the visual, which unites, and not on the printed or the spoken word, which divides.

We may say that this uniformity is superficial and this culture dull. We may try to escape at times. Tourism tries to get us to escape into the picturesque by emphasizing what is different and archaic in other countries, by showing us the old canals of Amsterdam and not the new docks of Rotterdam, the Beefeaters and cathedrals of England, and the tartans of Scotland. Nationalist movements also try to make us crawl back into a smaller world, by over-stressing outgrown customs and all but unintelligible languages. The denominations of the Church also offer their route of escape, by boasting of their age-old differences and their peculiar traditions. All these—tourism, nationalism, and denominationalism—are protests against the power and attraction of this new, uniform way of life. Their survival depends on their protest. But they at least do not make the mistake of thinking that this new way of life is superficial.

This new form of urban life evident in our replanned cities, our motorways, our airports, and our Olympic Games, is based on technical resources and skills unknown half a century ago. These share in determining the form and content of our educational system. These achievements are not only based on profound scientific knowledge but also for their carrying out depend on the technical training of many operatives and on new attitudes in countless other people. They depend on a common training and therefore on a basic common education. And this begins even to point the way to a common language. Already for air travel there has, of necessity, been evolved a common language for signals. Already in Britain and Europe we have uniform signs on roads. We have the beginnings of a rudimentary common language. It will certainly develop. A common language for all the world is not an impossibility.

This may be far from the common language of Pentecost. But for the first time in the world's history there is the possibility of one language throughout the world based on a common way of life, and are not a common language and a common way of life what Christians have long prayed for and held out in hope to men? Perhaps this is the way prayers are answered; by events catching up on our prayers, even though what has been achieved has come through technological advance. Man's progress has always come this way—through the discovery of the wheel, through the invention of printing, and of the internal-combustion engine. And if we prefer the stage-coach to the train (so long as we can afford to be passengers) and the galley to the plane (so long as we are not the slaves at the oars) who is being superficial?

But however we regard it, this expanding, or threatening, new common life is certainly a feature of our modern world. And it will spread rapidly.

And, fourthly, this modern, secular world has a new and fearful sense of its own *power* and its own responsibility. Man's development has always depended on his ability to use and to control material things. But up till the present age men have been only too well aware that they could control only a small part of the world, and then only intermittently. There was always the great unknown; uncontrollable, mysterious, the real decider of events. Men knew that they lived at the mercy of storms, drought, flood, and disease. And a great deal of the moral and religious teaching of the past was based on acceptance of and respect for the unknown. Human wisdom lay in man's recognition of his finite nature in front of the vast unknown. The authority of religion lay in its power to speak in the name of the unknowable. Today all this is gone. We know indeed that there are parts of life that we do not fully understand and which therefore we cannot control. But we expect that someday we shall attain this knowledge and this power. Men have lost the fear of the unknown, for the first time in human history. They have not got accustomed to this loss of fear. Indeed they feel a bit lost without it. What men fear today is not the unknown, but the known. Few of us live today in dread of lightning, but all Western men dread a nuclear war or someone's foolish mistake in international politics.

We know that the most appalling things that could happen are the things that men themselves could do. We also know that the most amazing things could happen if we wanted. As Margaret Mead, the eminent anthropologist, said in 1966 at the Geneva conference on Church and Society, 'There are a great many things that we have always wanted to do because of our love of God and of our neighbour. The point is that we now have the knowledge and power to do them if we will.' We are, for instance, aware of world hunger, as never before. This is not because the world has never known famine before this century. The world has always known famine, but it has taken it for granted as uncontrollable. We are aware of world hunger today because now we feel that if we pooled our knowledge and the resources of all the nations we could abolish it in a few decades. Ours is a new responsibility, and a new guilt.

The conquest of world hunger is the most obvious of the possibilities open to us in our new secular world. There is nothing to prevent the conquest of disease, ignorance, and war except our refusal to be grown-up and to use our knowledge, skills, and opportunities together for the common good. These are the terrifying responsibilities of power. And they are new.

This is an adult mood for mankind, different from the child's conviction that someone else is responsible and someone else will have to do something. This is why some people talk about the present time as man's coming of age. Some question the description because they say that men are still as childish as ever. But this is not the point. A youth does not suddenly become wise and responsible at eighteen or twenty-one. But he does become legally responsible for his own actions. He now has power if he wants to use it: the power to vote and to control his own affairs. And he is answerable for his own actions.

And this is a picture of man today. He can no longer claim the privileges of a child. He is no longer waiting to be given power and responsibility. He can no longer make the excuse of ignorance. He may not know what to do, but he questions the right of anyone who tries to tell him what to do on the authority of the unknown. He refuses to be dominated by the experience of former generations. He knows that he has to do things that they have never had to do. These are all features of adult life.

This parallel of man's situation today with that of a youth emerging from the tutelage of childhood into the responsibilities of adult life is illuminating, but it is also inadequate. The problem of youth emerging into adulthood is new and unique for each individual but it has been repeated for every generation for thousands of years. Man's coming of age now is something of which no previous generation has had any experience. Before now no men have known our freedom of power and knowledge, and our terrifying burden of responsibility. It is, therefore, no wonder that instead of feeling free to enter into their inheritance men today feel bewildered, lost in a world that is not their own, and talk about lack of identity, lack of community, and lack of purpose. We face questions—of danger and of opportunity—that men in the past have never faced. And we cannot follow the traditions and practices of the past. But this is our world. It offers greater opportunities and dangers than men have ever known before. And those of us whose faith is based on the need for radical change in men and in society should feel more at home with the new than with the old.

The bewildering changes of the world in which we now live are constantly presented to us by the instant impact of television, radio, and all the other forms of mass communication. Many of us may not be able to follow Marshall McLuhan in the coruscating abundance of his ideas, but most of us are aware that these new means of communication are not merely an extension of the printed word but represent something new that is happening to us and open new possibilities for our life together in the world. The events of the day and the way people react to them are before our eyes every day. Our vision of them influences our imaginations, our opinions and our actions : we don't quite know how.

We have described some of the main features of our modern secular world. We perhaps described them rather blatantly. But they are new and they do shriek at us, however much we try to hide from them. Whether we like it or not, the world is one, and limited in a way unknown before. It is also an open world in which we have now to live with other people, with all other people. And for the first time in the world's history we see emerging a uniform way of life which offers new possibilities for common thought and action. With these three radical changes men now have the power to determine their own destiny.

The problems that we now face in the world arise from these new and changing conditions. They can be reduced to the problems of race, hunger, and war. These problems cannot be solved without raising questions of right and wrong. But they can never be solved merely by ethical declarations. For involved in them are questions about the use of power and of political and economic co-operation. They can, indeed, be solved only in the secular world by men and women engaged in the secular life of the world. It is to the good of the Church that these questions are on the agenda of the councils and the assemblies of the Church. It is essential for the future of the world that they are on the agenda of the governments of the world.

In this chapter we have tried to show something of what is meant by the secular world. We have tried to show what is new and distinctive about it. Looked at in this way it may present to some a strange and even terrifying picture. Sometimes in the Church we are tempted to say that this is not our world. We resent its questions. We even suggest that these are not the right questions. We feel that the faith has to do with answers and not with questions. We don't want to see this new secular world.

Perhaps our first duty is to be honest. This is the world we live in. We don't know any other. Our children enjoy it : and so do we, despite all our fears and grumbles. We would not have liked to live at any other period of the world's history unless we could have been sure of occupying positions of extraordinary privilege. Before we protest about this modern world let us remember that we are as much a part of it as are its problems and its questions. We produce the questions just as we are the problems. We must take this world and its questions seriously. It is the only way in which we can take the Christian faith seriously.

3. Tomorrow's Theology and the Laity

Today's secular world raises questions for every one of us. These questions are practical. They have to do with our families, our jobs, our daily lives. New techniques in industry involve us in new relationships with other people. Increased mobility and the open society bring us into contact with people with whom previously we had little to do. Daily we face new questions as to how we should live. Some are old questions in new forms. Others are ones that men have never faced before. For these problems, such as birth control and the use of nuclear power, the past can offer no ready-made solutions. They come to us out of our new secular world and they demand immediate, practical answers if we are to make anything of our lives. But at the same time they bring haunting, fundamental, long-term questions about the world we live in, about our attitude to all other men and about the destiny of men on earth.

These are theological questions, though many of us would not recognize them as such. And today many men and women are uncomfortably aware of two things. One is that life presents them with problems which are immediate and seem insoluble, and yet have to be dealt with. The other is that it seems to be quite pointless to look to the clergy—or theology—for help. To them theology is remote, concerned with the past, and unintelligible. But like the character in Molière's play, who was surprised to learn that he was speaking prose all the time, the serious layman has to learn that *he is discussing theology most of the time*. For God is not, to quote Edwin Muir, 'three angry letters in a book'; nor by reading books on theology is one necessarily discussing true theology at all. One may be merely indulging in an abstruse intellectual exercise. When we discuss how we should regard the world we live in, how we should treat our neighbours in the street or at work, how we should educate our children; when we face such questions as our use of nuclear power or the chemical pollution of land and water, or the control of population, or racial discrimination, we are dealing with fundamental theological questions. And these are none the less so because the answers have to be found in action and not just in opinion.

Charles Williams has said that to him God is as certain as death : we might add 'and as indefinable and personal as life'. We are discussing God when we discuss seriously questions that are inescapable and seemingly insoluble, as well as when we are facing the flashes of certainty which come to all men at times in their lives. When we ask a question about the meaning of life or try to explain our experience, we are thinking about God. It might well be argued that men and women of this generation are far more theologically minded than those of previous generations, who were prepared to accept beliefs without questioning. Certainly there is far more thinking about God—for negative thinking is still thinking—than in the past generations, and certainly more criticism of our thinking.

There is a tragic gap between the profound and unsatisfied questioning of ordinary men and women and what they take to be the accepted teaching of the Church. This appears to them to be something that they have to accept at second hand, without verification in their secular lives. It is perfectly true that many lay people are glad to accept this remote theology as a means of escape from their life in the world. It is also true that most clergy would deny that there is any intentional gap. But the gap is there so far as most lay people are concerned; and it explains the very real reaction against theology by many people, especially young people.

There are, fortunately, theologians who have raised the standard of revolt against the old theology. There are many of them. And they are of all kinds. (For those who are particularly interested, a special list of some of their books is given in the Bibliography.) Of many of them the criticism could still be made that their books are written to be read by fellow theologians. They are more concerned to demolish old conceptions than to find new ways of expression intelligible to modern men. Probably the first stage has to be negative. Perhaps the academic theologian can never be creative. Perhaps he has to await the creative contribution of the laymen—of the artist, the scientist, the politician.

This is perhaps why J. A. T. Robinson's book, *Honest to God*, is still the most important of these rebellious books. It was not the first, but it was the first one that somehow managed to cross the gap and to be read by ordinary lay people. They may not have understood all its references. But it did two things for them. It gave them liberty to question. The great release that *Honest to God* brought to many people was not through a sudden understanding of new truths, but the comfort of knowing that it was a quite respectable thing for a member of the Church to say 'I don't believe this,' or 'I can't really swallow that.' And this is an important step forward. New understanding of the truth generally begins with the repudiation of an accepted statement as quite unsatisfactory.

And the other thing that *Honest to God* and the other books which try to explain the meaning of secular Christianity have done is to indicate to the layman that they take his world seriously.

These books have opened dusty windows and let in some light. But there are three great difficulties that the Church's thinking has to surmount if it is to develop a theology that speaks to men's condition today and to which lay men and women can contribute. The first difficulty is that of language. The second is our changed attitude to authority. And the third is our reluctance to experiment in new forms of expression.

Language is the initial obstacle. Many people have an uneasy feeling that the words common in theological books and popular in sermons and prayers not only mean nothing to most of the people who hear them, but mean almost as little to those who utter them. Words like atonement, sacrifice, redemption, immanence, and transcendence are the worn coins of a discarded currency. Many people become frustrated and irritated by the insistence of theologians and preachers on trying to explain these outworn terms instead of finding contemporary means of expressing essential truths. Such a refusal to search seriously for forms of thought and expression that are relevant to the new world in which we live is very liable to be interpreted as meaning that the faith belongs to the past and not to the present. It is sometimes justified by the assertion that the faith must not compromise with the spirit of the age. But this is to be most unfair to the Church in the past. When the Church has been most aware of its mission it has always found a way of talking in the secular language of the time.

When Paul went out into the Roman world he abandoned much of the language of the Old Testament, except when he was speaking to Jews. He spoke to men in terms of their own experience. Slavery was the economic basis of their life. Those who were free men knew that the life of their society depended on others being their slaves. Those who were slaves had only one hope: to be free. And freedom could only be bought at a price. So, because slavery was a real thing, Paul made freedom the basis of his preaching of Christ. He interpreted Christ in terms of bondage and freedom. He spoke of Christ's work as redemption; of our being bought at a price. He saw the hope of the world as the glorious liberty of the children of God in which all men and all things would have their place.

When, centuries later, slavery in its old form was a thing unknown in Christendom, the Church explained the faith in different terms. What men now knew was the feudal order, with its social gradations and its clear scheme of duties to those above and responsibilities to those below, and therefore with definite views of guilt and punishment. So the theologians of the Middle Ages and of the Reformation expounded the faith in terms of feudal relationships—of substitution, punishment, and duty.

Today slavery is unknown and feudalism is dead. But theologians still think it is possible to talk about the faith in terms of redemption and atonement. The laity's refusal to listen to all this is by the power of the Holy Spirit.

But don't let us think that all we have to do is to look round for the equivalents of slavery and feudalism in our contemporary life. Our problem is much more difficult than that. Men in the Roman world knew what slavery was. Mediaeval men knew what feudalism was. They had been the accepted patterns of men's lives for generations, familiar and unchanging. We do not live in that kind of stable world. We live in a world that is rapidly changing, that raises questions to which we have no adequate answers, in which men face problems that men have never faced before. How are men to live at peace in a world that is already becoming too small for them? How are we to control the use of nuclear power which is in the hands of some nations? How are we to take the appalling responsibility of deciding by birth control and genetic science what nations or what classes or what types of men are to increase, and which to die out? And who are we, who are going to decide?

These questions come to us from the modern world, not from the Bible or the past. They are secular questions and demand as contemporary an answer now as Paul gave for his day, or the mediaeval and Reformation theologians did for theirs. No one would claim that we have begun to find the answer. Our contention is that we shall only begin to find it as laymen begin to be concerned in the search. But to go on using the old terms of slavery and feudalism is to reduce theology to the level of fairy tales.

It is not only obscurity of language that makes so much of the Church's theology repulsive. It is also its irrelevance. Men find the language of the scientist no easier to understand, but they endeavour to read what the scientists are saying because they know it means something to the scientist and is concerned with the world we must live in today and tomorrow. It is not a matter of finding simple words and simple pictures to express profound ideas, as clergymen so often seem to think. They think that if they can only be simple enough people will understand. But this is the approach of an advertising agency. It has never been the way in which the Gospel has been effectively presented to men. The Gospel has made an impact when it has been seen in terms of the most difficult and controversial topics of the day, as when Paul expressed the faith in terms of race and sex and class, the seemingly insoluble problems of the Roman world. Men are now so indifferent to and irritated by much of what the Church appears to be saying because of its irrelevance to modern life. And what the Church *appears* to be saying is often much more influential than what some wise men in the Church are actually writing!

And deeper than men's irritation with antiquated language is men's radically changed attitude to authority. What may be challenged now is not the theologians failure to say anything relevant but their right to say anything at all. This questioning goes far deeper than we often think. And it is the awareness of this that makes church leaders often suspicious of and antagonistic to any kind of lay movement or training in the Church. They see these as a challenge to their traditional authority, and they are right. We can go forward with the development of self-education for lay men and women only if we realize this: the old idea of authority in the Church will be increasingly challenged. If there is to be any reformation in the Church and if the Church is to fulfil any kind of mission in the world of tomorrow, it is here that the battle will have to be fought.

'Authority' is a sacred word in the Church and 'revolt' has an unpleasant sound. But this revolt against authority has to be taken very seriously if we wish to understand the world in which we live and the crisis of theology today.

In its simplest and basic form it is a questioning of the claims of others to enforce their views on us. This is no new thing. It is basic both to the Christian faith and to modern science. It inspired Paul to break with the tradition in which he had been brought up. It inspired Luther and Wesley—and, indeed, every theologian who has made a contribution of note to the thinking of the Church. It has inspired every act of discovery and invention. These pioneers did what the ordinary men of their time were not prepared to do—they questioned the authority of their teachers and elders.

This rejection of the absolute claims of authority is now as evident inside the churches as it is outside. Men are reluctant to accept a statement just because it is spoken with the authority of a church or a party. A report of the World Council of Churches, or for that matter an encyclical from Rome, will be accepted only as it appeals to the reason of people both inside and out-

side the Church. One of the aims and one of the achievements of modern education has been to instil in the
minds of men a questioning of irrational or arbitrary
authority.

The authority that they question is not the right of
church or party to express opinions and to try to per-
suade others to accept them, but their desire to decide
how other people should live their lives. It is persecution
to use your position to impose your views on other men,
to prevent them from doing what they want to do (apart
from blatantly antisocial behaviour), to force them to
conform to patterns of social behaviour which they do
not accept. The popularity of Robert Burns in Scotland
and now elsewhere is due not so much to his poetry as to
the resentment expressed in his poetry and in his life
against the persecuting authority of the Church. The
Church, which likes to recite 'Blessed are ye when men
shall persecute you,' finds it very difficult to realize that
in the eyes of a good many people today it is the Church
that persecutes rather than is persecuted.

This is the basic, modern, unsophisticated revolt that
has to be taken seriously, especially if we take education
seriously. Modern man is bound to be a rebel. The only
alternative is to submit to being a slave.

And thirdly, reinforcing our questioning of authority,
there is the awareness that our knowledge of the world
is changing so fast that any positive or dogmatic statement is of only temporary validity. This is partly due to
the influence of science, which bases its work on constant criticism of its accepted beliefs. It is also due to our
facing situations in our ordinary lives that men never
had to face before. Most of us are aware of a greater
need to learn than to teach. The Church has been for so
long a teaching authority that it finds it very hard to
acquire a learning function. And this is where the laity
comes in, for the layman has been trained in his secular
life to learn while the clergyman has been conditioned to

instruct. Professor Donald MacKinnon said in a distinguished broadcast: 'The apostle is able to teach only so far as he is also learning.' And he went on to explain how the ecclesiastic was afraid of this because it challenged his security, which was built on his 'withdrawing himself from the common way of men and women, from both the constant and the transient conditions of their lives'.[1] But it is from our transient lives that we learn and in them that we have to act.

The fears of the ecclesiastic are summed up in his suspicion of the word 'new', especially if applied to theology or morality. Yet if theology is to be relevant, it must always be new. The fundamental faith that it is trying to express is unchanging. But the form in which it is expressed must always be contemporary, inadequate, changing. It is strange how men who see the need of new thinking and new structures in every other aspect of their lives can be so horrified at the idea of new theological or moral thinking. It is inconceivable that when we are thinking in new terms about the material world and when we know that we must find new ways of living with all the other inhabitants of the world, we should not have to find new ways of thinking about the world and new ways of behaving to each other. It is inevitable that there should be a new morality and a new theology. The question is, what are they to be like?

We are not, of course, waiting for new thinking. We don't have to wonder how we begin. In our ordinary secular lives we are already thinking in new ways. We could not do our jobs if we weren't. Many of us are in jobs that didn't exist fifty years ago—electronic engineers, TV producers, town planners. Many of us who are in longer established jobs know that what we do and how we talk about our jobs would be unintelligible to

1. Reprinted in *The Listener*, March 23, 1967, p. 384: and in *The Stripping of the Altars* by Donald MacKinnon, Fontana Library, 1969, p. 56.

those who worked in them a hundred years ago. We know that whatever our jobs are we must take a new look at them and at how we train young people for them. Even if we never think of using the words, we are dealing with theology and with morality—with our attitude to the world and with our attitude and behaviour to other people. And our thinking is new.

The need to find new ways of behaviour is more obvious to people than the need for new ways of thinking about the world—the need for a new morality is probably clearer than the need for a new theology. Those who are afraid of anything new try to frighten others by the use of the word 'permissive', but the so-called 'new morality' is not in its origins so very new. It might be more to the point to ask what the old morality was.

To find the origins of the morality that is under challenge we must go back, not to the New Testament, but to the mediaeval idea of Christendom : to the picture of a besieged citadel, defending itself against the attacks of infidels and pagans and maintained by an authoritative discipline, military and ecclesiastical. This morality was based on two assumptions not found in the New Testament : that war is justified and that punishment is necessary.

Christendom justified war and made it holy. 'After the triumph of the Cross,' writes Steven Runciman, 'after the Empire had become Christendom, ought not its citizens to take up arms for its welfare? The Eastern Church thought not. . . . The Western point of view was less enlightened. . . . The code of chivalry that was developing gave prestige to the military hero; and the pacifist acquired a disrepute from which he has never recovered.'[2] From this followed many things; the author-

2. *A History of the Crusades*, Vol. I, Cambridge University Press, 1951, pp. 83–4.

ity of the Church imposed by ecclesiastical and military law, crusades against heretics, the Inquisition, an emphasis on the language of warfare in our hymns and prayers, even much of our talking about evangelistic campaigns and crusades.

The other foundation of the morality of Christendom was the idea of punishment. It affected much more than the morality of Christendom. It was basic to its theology. Punishment was fundamental in the thinking of feudal society. It was the means by which feudal relationships were maintained. The mediaeval conception of justice demanded that the cost must be paid. This was reinforced by the theology of the Church with its teaching on substitution, propitiation, and punishment.

The foundations of the old morality were shaken when in the last century men began to question the morality of war and the place of punishment in the treatment of offenders. The movements for the renunciation of war and for the reformation of the treatment of prisoners and delinquents went back beyond the teaching of Christendom to the teaching of the New Testament, and were based on a recovered sense of the integrity of the person. And, of course, since then this movement has been reinforced by the growth of our psychological knowledge, by the horror of the two world wars and the threat of nuclear war, by the extension of education, by the new freedom put into people's hands by birth control and, not least, by the emancipation of women. It has been a change from authority to freedom : from the idea of authority, enforced by sanctions, to the idea of the individual's right to decide for himself what is right and to the conception of the function of society being to protect the individual's freedom.

The fact that many of those who struggled for the new morality have not been Christians should not blind us to the Christian origins of the movement, and the biblical nature of its aims. We must, however, certainly admit that many reformers have been opposed by those inside the Church who have not mentally moved away from the idea of Christendom. These traditionalists still think of the Church as under attack. They are on the defensive. They will have nothing to do with those who are not professed Christians. They want to defend their separateness, their distinctiveness and especially their privileges. Indeed their privileges are all they have to defend. Today we know that their picture is all a charade. We're not besieged. We're not under attack. We're in the open with other men. We're back in the much healthier position of the Christians of the second century as described for us in the 'Letter to Diognetus': 'Christians cannot be distinguished from the rest of the human race by country or language or customs. They do not live in cities of their own; they do not use a peculiar form of speech; they do not follow an eccentric manner of life.'

A society under siege can find a justification for a rigidly imposed moral code. In an open society, where life is shared with men and women of many opinions, moral conduct has to find a basis in reason and agreement. The Christian has not only to square his actions with his faith; he has also to work out his actions with other people. This makes a new morality inevitable.

A repudiation of the use of force and a recognition of the integrity of the person both lead to a new openness in our treatment of moral questions. This applies particularly to the new relationships of men and women in society, to the relations of young and old and to the relationships of people working together in an organization of any kind. It can no longer be a matter of codes of conduct to be imposed, but of patterns of behaviour to be approved.

The need for a new morality arises from extreme dissatisfaction with the old codes of conduct. The need for a new theology arises partly from the inadequacy of mediaeval theology to speak to modern conditions but even more from the colossal omissions of that theology. The theology of Christendom had little to say about the world of other men and therefore little to say about the mission of the Church. It was the theology of a static, limited community. Its aim was to maintain the life of a tight little community bounded by the frontiers of Christendom. It was not interested in the life and thought of those outside. It did not share Paul's ambition to reach the ends of the earth and his desire to stand where no Christian had stood before. It did not share his interest in what men of other races were thinking. So, when the walls began to be broken down by exploration and men's curiosity about the rest of the world in trade and in the desire of some in the Church to take the Gospel to those in other lands, not in war but in service, the theologians did not know what to say. Or rather they knew that they could only say 'No'. The classical theologians from after Augustine's time until Calvin's had never dealt with the subject. Christianity was for Christendom. The other parts of the world had their own religions and had nothing to do with the Christians' God. So the missionary movement of the eighteenth and nineteenth centuries was not started by the official churches or with the blessing of the theologians. It was started by lay groups.

Two questions face men today: how are they to use the material world? and, how are they to live together with all other men? These are new in that our knowledge of the material world is new and changing, and new in that for the first time we have to live with all other men. These are immediate questions that men face when they go to work or when they watch the news on TV. But they are the questions on which traditional theology has little to say. The Church in the last century and a half has been fumbling towards a theology of humanity and a theology of Christian mission. It will discover this theology only through those who are engaged with others in the work of the world.

The task of the Church is not to defend its faith but to find its faith; not to try to hold people in loyalty to outworn statements of the faith but to try to find what an ever-living faith means for tomorrow. We cannot believe in a creative purpose for the world (and this is what we mean by saying that we believe in 'God, the Father, Almighty, Creator'), and in the meaning of it given in the life and teaching of Jesus and in the present working of his spirit in us, unless we believe that the future matters much more than the past and that we have to be alive in our understanding as in our obedience. But this is the business of the whole Church. For the theology of the Church comes out of the life and experience of the Church and not out of books. And this thinking cannot be done without the laity. It certainly cannot be done by the clergy alone. Their education gives them little training for the task, and their past theological thinking has not helped them to share in the thinking of the laity. The working-out of Christian theology about the world today and the life of all men together in it *has to come out of experience of that life*, and therefore must be done primarily by lay people with, if possible, the co-operation and understanding of the clergy.

The theology of tomorrow depends on the laity. No one would pretend that they are ready for their task. It will be a long, slow task. The temptation will be to take short cuts. Inevitably we will be tempted to start where the theologians are. We will be inclined to think that what we need are textbooks and study outlines. We have to start very much further back. We have to begin where men are today, with their questions and their experience. But this is to go back to the Gospel.

Many laymen would put their questions simply, if pointedly. They want to know in what sense they can call this world God's creation. Is this modern, secular world, in which they live and work, according to God's purpose for the world? In their service of it are they serving God?

They want to know whether a man's personal world —home and work, children and neighbours, his hopes and fears, joy and death—has any significance in God's purpose for the world, or any meaning at all.

And then, though they may not express it so openly, they wonder whether the life and teaching of Jesus have any significance for their ordinary lives and for this secular world today.

These are, indeed, the deepest theological questions that men can ask. And answers at second hand are of no use to men today. They are suspicious of time-worn answers. They want answers that start by speaking to their own limited but personal experience. The demand that men are making today is to be allowed to ask their own questions and to test the validity of their own answers, and this questioning by lay people demands of the Church a radical scrutiny of all its traditional teaching and a willingness to get to the root of people's questions. This sometimes means being patient with people's foolishly phrased questions and taking what lies behind them seriously. It also involves the expectation of finding new light from them and the hope of the greater things in which Jesus promised still to reveal himself. Such a willingness to jettison familiar words and to experiment with new forms of expression will inevitably lead to a discovery of the few radical beliefs on which the Christian faith is built and to a fresh understanding of them.

And perhaps we've not to be too much concerned about words. Certainly not theological words and their definitions. Perhaps the way we discover these elemental truths is through action and through art. This is what lay men and women must do if they are given, or can take, their freedom. They must resist any pressure from the clergy simply to build up a rival system of fixed theology to place against the old. They must go on continually asking awkward questions and acting out their own answers.

John L. Casteel sums up well the issues raised in this chapter: 'If creativity in theoretical science is becoming more and more a function of groups of scientists and less and less the activity of the solitary genius, the same process may be assumed to have its use in the formation of a new and relevant religious understanding. Still further if theology arises out of reflection upon experience, understood in faith, a fresh and vital emergence of theology may wait for the contribution that might be made by lay men and women, as they describe and reflect upon the implications of their living experience.'[3]

3. *The Creative Role of International Groups in the Church Today*, edited by John L. Casteel, Association Press, New York, 1968.

4. Worship and the Laity

The Christian lives his life in the world. In this he is the same as all other people. No one can live his life anywhere else. What is peculiar to the Christian is his identification with the world. A Christian is tied to the world by all the ties by which a man can be tied. He is different from other men in that he knows that he is so tied and sees his faith in terms of this. Unlike Plato, who believed that our knowledge of this world was only of shadows, the Christian believes that this is God's world through which he speaks to men. Unlike the followers of the great religions of the East, who regard the material world as either evil or unreal, the Christian knows the world of God's creation as good. He confesses that by his faith he is called to serve the world.

The ordinary layman, who has not been trained to great subtlety of thought, sees the point of his faith in love, not in detachment, and in unity, not in division. He knows that the place of his service must be in the world. He would like to think of the Church as the herald and the instrument of God's purpose for all men. He wants to live out his faith in action and in worship. But he finds himself up against great difficulties. Action becomes uncertain and worship confused.

One of the main difficulties is that today we are all too apt to spend our time making divisions between men on political, racial, and religious grounds. In the Church we've spent an inordinate amount of time in making and defending divisions: between the Church and the world, religion and politics, soul and body, spirit and matter. Much of our theological thinking is spent on elaborating and proclaiming our divisions in the Church : between Catholic and Protestant, Anglican and Presbyterian, East and West. We even pretend that these divisions are confessions of faith and not of failure.

The ground of the Christian faith is unity, not division. Jesus refused to recognize the divisions made by the men of his time : between the religious and the non-religious, between men and women, between Jew and Samaritan, between good and bad. His great offence was that he disregarded the barriers that men had erected to keep them apart from other men. And Paul, when he went out to declare the faith that he had found in Jesus, claimed that Jesus had broken down the walls of division between men and, therefore, between man and God. He said that in so doing Jesus had made men one : that in this new unity there was a new humanity. This was the basis of the mission of the Church to the world.

It's very easy for us in the Church to appropriate Jesus to ourselves, to think that we must bring other men into our company if they are to meet him, and to quote Paul's words, 'Christ died for us,' without the words that go before, 'While we were yet sinners.' For it was before anyone could be called a Christian that Jesus lived and died. Jesus never saw a Christian. He knew only men. And he was not a Christian. He was a man.

The Christian faith can never be tied up in a tidy parcel. It is always slopping out into the whole of life, to the irritation of those with tidy minds. It is always refusing to be confined to the limits of private life, to the annoyance of its enemies. It continually idenifies itself with other men, to the annoyance of its jealous friends. It is intertwined with all of life, as an intrinsic part of it. It interprets all of life : the life of the non-Christian as much as the life of the Christian.

This is why Christians are always involved in the world. This is why sometimes they are accused of interfering unwarrantably in the affairs of other people. This is why they cannot complain if others interfere in their affairs. The wall of separation is down, however hard we try to build it up again.

The Christian is, thus, in a special relationship to the world—to the material world and to other men. It is not that he is any more or any less part of creation than other men. His special relationship lies in his knowing that he is part of the world and that for him the world finds its purpose in the glory of God. He does not feel himself, therefore, to be the victim of material forces, nor is he a rebel against them. He also knows that he shares life with all other men. He is not trying to distinguish himself from them. He is not afraid of others; he knows that he shares life with them whoever they are. His identification with others is without conditions. He does not say he will be at one with other men if they will do this or believe that. He knows that he shares life with them because Jesus shares life with them. This is the liberty of Christian men. This is what Paul meant by the liberty wherewith Christ has made us free (Galatians 5.1). It is a freedom from law, by which we do things because we're told to do them; a freedom from ourselves or our concern solely with ourselves; a freedom from fear. This is how a Christian knows he is called to live, however much he knows that he fails.

The life he lives is life in this physical, secular world— the ordinary material world of ordinary material men. This common earthy life which he shares with all men is what is meant by the expression 'life in the body of Christ'. The life of Christians is lived in the world, just as the life of Jesus was lived in the world, in all the involvement of his daily life, with all the attachments of his life.

The Christian life is summed up in the word 'communion'. It is the key both to his action and to his worship. Its root is the word 'common', and 'common' means 'shared by all'. Communion is the act or the ex-

perience of sharing with others. It can mean talking together, conversation, communication. It always means
being in contact with others. The word comes from
Latin. Its English equivalent is 'fellowship'. Communion
emphasizes the things shared. Fellowship emphasizes the
fact of personal sharing. Both are sides of the same thing.
Both emphasize the fullness of the sharing. Communion
is the opposite of what is private, exclusive, individual.

When we put the word 'holy' before it we do not
cancel out the original meaning of 'common'. We are
not saying that some things that are common can be
lifted out of this commonness into a realm that is special
and different. We are saying that the *common is holy so
long as we keep it really common and do not make any
private, individual, exclusive claim upon it. The* word
'holy' means whole, perfect. We use it of our sharing of
the gift of Jesus' life because this was freely shared with
all men and is therefore the perfect representation of
that common sharing which is the Christian life. In it we
are at one with him and with all men.

This is the life into which God's people are brought by
baptism and to which they are committed by their confirmation. It is the life of the body of Christ in the world.
We are afraid to say 'the life of the Church' because the
word 'church' so often evokes in the minds of ordinary
men and women the picture of special buildings and
separated groups and religious activities, with Holy
Communion seen as a specially religious action instead
of the sign and seal of common life. This is a complete
parody of the Church, which is the common people of
Christ set in the common life of the world, to be lost in it
as salt is lost and to serve it as a lamp serves all in a
room.

As we are in this book considering the education of
lay Christians, it is perhaps well to think for a moment
how relevant the conception of the common life is to all
education. An infant finds in the common life around

him both an assurance of that trust in the world around him which he expresses in his demand for food, and that need for affection which is his feeling after God. A growing child finds in his need of companions the proof of his need to share life with other people. An adolescent knows the challenge—and sometimes the refusal—of the giving of himself. All his growing life is set in this awareness of and struggle to find—and sometimes to resist—the life of the body to which he knows he must belong.

It is of this life of the body that Holy Communion is the symbol.

This is why Holy Communion often has meaning for a child even before he is allowed by the discipline of his Church to share in it. This is why it is important for children to be present at the celebration of the sacrament, that they by seeing what is done may understand the meaning of the life they live with other people.

By its use of material things—food and drink—Holy Communion ties us to the material world. This is the first visible impression that the sacrament makes on those who watch. And this must have been the impression made on the disciples in the upper room. When Jesus took bread and said, 'This is my body,' he was saying something about the bread as clearly as he was saying something about his body. Indeed it would be on the bread that the disciples' eyes would be fixed, while in their minds they would be wondering how *this* could be his body. And when he took the cup and said, 'This cup is the new covenant in my blood,' it would be on the cup that their eyes were fixed, this common cup from which they all drank—the symbol of the life he had shared with them, the life he was now giving up for them.

It was common bread, taken from the table. And bread is not merely the product of natural growth. It is the product of man's labour. The same is true of the wine in the cup. Sometimes we are inclined to think that we find God by getting away as far as we can from man. We think that we find him in solitude and that we might expect wild honey and clear running water to be the symbols of his gifts to men. But we know God in our life with other men and the symbols of Communion are the bread of a woman's baking and the wine of man's making. It is a reminder, too, that men are a part of nature : that the way of God's creation is not a wilderness but a garden and its end a city and not a solitude. In Communion we accept and rejoice in our place in the world of nature. This is evident in the fact of bread and wine.

But this is not all. The bread is broken and the wine is poured out. By this we are linked with the life and death of Jesus—and with the suffering of all other men. For whenever we break bread, whenever we eat and drink, whenever we have a meal at home or in a canteen or in a restaurant, we are always showing forth the death of other men—those who have died to produce the food or to bring it to us, those who have been killed for men's greed for it, those who starve because men do not want to share. In Communion we are tied to all from which we daily seek to untie ourselves—the pain, the cruelty, the shame of men. We are tied to it because we know that Jesus accepted all this. He took the bread and the cup as the symbols of the life he lived and shared with men. Because we know that what Jesus did in his life and death is the most revealing thing that has ever happened in the world, we can face the fact of our own sufferings and other men's. We have no easy solutions to satisfy our minds; but we know in our hearts something of the mystery and the glory of life.

And there is a third way by which the Communion ties us to life. The bread which is broken and given to us is always shared with others. Communion is not only our acceptance of the common mercies of life. Nor is it only, though it is supremely, the mystery of our participation in the love of God in Jesus. It is also our act of sharing with other men. Most of us would see as very real this sharing with those we meet at the same table in our local church. Sometimes this sharing finds visible expression in the passing of bread and cup from hand to hand, or in the sharing of an ordinary meal before or after the service, or in the kiss of peace as in the Church of South India, or a handshake in a modern Roman Catholic mass. Many would see this sharing as extending in imagination to all who elsewhere celebrate the same Communion. Most of us would argue that this sharing transcends the denominational barriers that often prevent us joining in this service with other Christians.

But does this sharing stop there? Is our Communion not with all men? If I can say, 'Christ died for me,' does it not follow with equal surprise that he died for all men? My sharing of his life binds me in fact, and not just in love, to all other men.

Communion is, thus, the key to life. Its reference is to all life, not just to religious life. It gives meaning to all that happens to a man from birth, whether he be a Christian or not. It is not just a peculiar religious ceremony, a ritual to be observed at least once a year, a sign of membership of the Church. It is the truth about life : the truth about people and things and about a man's relationship to them. For life is communion.

It is also the key to worship.

Life means action and worship. These are the two things that make human life distinctive. We cannot have human life without work. We cannot survive without it. We cannot progress without it. It is work that gives man control of the material world. It is work that brings him into co-operative relation with his fellows. It is in work that he is made in the image of God. And without worship he cannot find meaning in his life. Without something to worship he cannot know the meaning of pain and frustration, glory, and hope.

The difference for a man who calls himself a Christian

is that he knows why he works and why he worships, but worship cannot be discussed apart from life. Worship cannot be regarded as an activity in which a man engages quite apart from his daily life.

Many lay men and women find the worship of the Church increasingly dissatisfying. Of course there are some who find in worship all that they desire. They are fortunate in their place of worship, or fortunate in the education they have received in worship; or they may just be fortunate in their temperament. There are also some who want worship to be an escape, who don't want it to be demanding, who relish it just because it is out of date. But there are a great many more who want to worship, but who are frustrated by the irrelevancy of much of the Church's worship. It is for these people that this book is written, for with them lies the future of the Church in the next few decades.

Their difficulty lies in the lack of connection between the common life of the world and the worship of the Church.

This is seen in various ways.

The form and content of worship as we know it today in our churches seems to have little to do with our daily life, except in its domestic and leisure aspects. It has to do with our private lives—with what we do in our homes, with some of our leisure-time relationships and with our private use of money. But it seems to have little to do with how we make our money; and how we live and work with others in our daily work and in our political life.

This is not always apparent to those trained to conduct worship; for they know that the form of the liturgy, the contents of the psalms and ancient hymns, and the older prayers of the Church do *not* express this private view of worship. But to the ordinary worshipper the psalms and canticles of praise (which in fact acclaim the whole universe as created by God and existing for his praise) are not understood as having anything to do with the world of nuclear science and modern industry and politics which he knows.

Again worship, as the layman commonly experiences it, seems to emphasize division from other men and separation from the daily life he shares with them. There is the feeling, nourished by a special building and a peculiar language, that worship means withdrawal into another world, in which the affairs of daily life cannot find a place. Worship divides him off from the ordinary companions of his daily life. He finds it uncomfortable to talk to them about his life in church, even to those who also go to church. Participation in worship does not seem to lead him into a feeling of communion with other men. Sometimes he can hold to the practice of worship by making it a very private, and sometimes almost a secret, rite. But most lay people are not like this. They simply feel worship more and more unreal.

Thirdly, the forms and the language become increasingly meaningless and strange to those whose thinking is moulded and conditioned by their life in the secular world. The words of many of our hymns have acquired a sacred aura and inherited associations which are unknown to those who are not familiar with them—and who are being trained in secular education to ask what words *mean*. It seems strange to a man of today to sing,

'Change and decay in all around I see,'

when the change he sees is the demolition of slums and the erection of new multi-storey flats and the making of new roads. It is not only the words that sound archaic; the ideas that come through the hymns, the prayers and the sermons seem to express withdrawal from the world, condemnation of any attempts to find a new way of life for the world, and satisfaction with the cosiness of a contracting area of private life. Here again the clergy find it difficult to appreciate the discomfort and even the torture endured by some of their people in church. They have been educated to put into the words that they use the meanings that they originally had, in Hebrew or Greek or in Elizabethan English. Many of them are indeed as dissatisfied with archaic language as are some of the laity, and express their rebellion in provocative sermons—to their own satisfaction but often to the confusion of the laity who want to know why clergy still use such words if this is how they feel. The laity have too often only one means of protest; to stay away from church.

Worship is far too essential to the life of the Church for it to be left in its present mess. It is not enough to try new hymns and to use new translations of the Bible and to get lay men and women to take a more active and responsible part in the services. These are important reforms and they must be done. But they could all be done efficiently and superficially—without any real change in the laity's understanding of how worship has a vital connection with their daily lives.

When we get away from the details of how we worship and get down to the question of what we are doing in worship, then there are four points which we must consider.

The first point is that in worship we recapture our vision of what the world really is. We free our minds from our selfish concerns and our fixed assumptions and values. We stop for a moment in wonder. We try to think what it means to say that in the world there is creativity and purpose and in life there is glory. We see that this is what Jesus means for us and what God is. We know that we are called to share in this creativity and thus we have part in the future of the world.

Secondly : this, the divine side of our worship, finds its climax and its fullest expression in the sacraments. In the sacraments, through material things—water, bread, wine—we know our bodily participation in God's action in the world. Because of this the sacraments have relevance for our secular life in the world rather than for our religious life in the Church. They tie us to the material world; they commit us to all men whom Christ called brothers. The sacraments are, therefore, of particular importance to us precisely as we are concerned with the work of the world.

The third point is this: worship has not only this divine side, it has also its human side. Worship is something we do as men. It is indeed a peculiarly human activity—a fully human activity. We sometimes talk of a service of worship in church as the 'divine office' of the Church. If we mean by this the worship of God this is all right, but it is an awkward way of saying it. If we mean that there is something peculiarly divine in what we do, then surely we are mistaken. The only service of the Christian to which we could ever apply the adjective 'divine' is the life to which Christ calls his people. The divine office of the Church is in its life of love. When Paul talks of being in Christ or of Christ being in us, it is to this life that he refers. This is what we do in Christ's name and not in our own: this is what we can do only by his spirit. The offering of our worship is quite a different service. *It is the one thing we do as men in our own name:* the one thing we can only do in our own name; which we cannot do in Christ's name. For basically it is our expression of thanks and praise for Jesus Christ and all that he means for us. Because it is a human activity, which we do consciously, deliberately, and joyfully, we can and must bring into it all that we have and are: our thinking, our music, our art. This is the justification for our use of the arts in worship. Our worship is our fullest human activity.

The fourth point is that worship is in the name of all creation. Christian worship is made in the name of all created things. The worship of a small country church is not merely the worship of a few people gathered together; it is the worship of the whole Church. In the same way the worship of the whole Church is not merely the worship of all Christian people. It has a cosmic significance. It is the worship of the whole creation—of earth and heaven. In worship the Church expresses the praise that creation 'voiceless sings', the praise that all men dimly feel after but cannot utter. In the celebration of Holy Communion we say that 'with angels and archangels and all the company of heaven, we worship and adore'—but not only with these : surely also with earth and all created things, with all men and women and children we worship and adore. We, in the Church, know something of what we are doing : why we worship and adore. But even when we do it we know that we don't know fully or even adequately. We are glad that our imperfect understanding can be taken up in a renewing act of praise. In the same way our worship must be seen as an act in which others have their place, even though they do not know it.

We need experiments in music, words, and forms to make worship relevant to daily life. But these experiments will prove superficial and ephemeral if they are concerned only with music, words, and forms. What we need, even more, is a recovery of the human meaning and width of worship, and a discovery of new corporate ways of living Christ's life of divine service.

In this lay men and women have a primary responsibility. If the worship of tomorrow is to be relevant and vital it will only be so because the laity are intent to discover the way of corporate action in the secular world and bring this into the worship of the Church. They alone can do this.

It is obvious to at least some church leaders that the laity have primary responsibility for action in the world. Their primary responsibility in worship is not so generally recognized. And this is mainly for two reasons.

One is that generally in the Church the emphasis has

been on the forms of worship rather than on the nature of worship. And the forms, being historical, depend for their understanding on scholars. In recent years a great work has been done by scholars in interpreting and simplifying traditional forms of worship. Our forms of worship are being freed from much that is ornate and archaic in traditional language and are thus being made more intelligible to men today. But even so worship still seems to depend on the work of scholars; it still needs to be explained by the clergy. Worship thus becomes something at second hand for the laity. An action which has to be explained to men and in which they have to be led can lack the element of spontaneity which is essential for worship.

The other follows from this. Because church worship is something that has to be explained, it does not generally arise out of our daily lives. There are occasions when worship does spring from a man's daily life: when he is married, when he brings a child for baptism, or when death has struck him closely. Then he knows something of what worship is. But, strangely, he finds sometimes that the clergy have rather a contempt for worship that is so obviously useful. Worship, he gathers, should not have anything to do with the secular world. But he knows that he has to do with the secular world. He lives in it. It is his world. He is aware that in the secular world he has to express his faith and hope and love; that if he does not he has no right to be working in it.

This barrier between church worship and daily life has to be broken down if worship is to become alive for him and for the Church tomorrow. Worship, if it is to mean anything at all, must be immediate, at first hand. He who is a spectator is not a worshipper. To talk about attending worship is a kind of blasphemy. It is probably true that an illiterate, peasant congregation participates in worship more by the ear and the eye than with a critical and rational mind. But this is participation all the same. For an educated congregation such participation is impossible : with a denial of the mind it becomes merely attendance. And worship is something that a man does, not something he watches someone else do. It must be the free, immediate response of the whole man, just as his response in love and action must be.

He can respond as a full person only as he brings his whole world with him. He alone can directly infuse worship with the reality of God's action in the world now. It is probably true that the minister can do much to help him to understand the full meaning of God's action in the past, but he with all his fellow lay men and women can certainly interpret God's action in the world today (always remembering that the clergy have also their lay responsibilities and experience in the secular world, and therefore their contribution to make here too).

Worship can never be merely the re-acting of an old play, even when the words are modernized and the audience made to participate. Worship must be the immediate expression of the faith of men and women in the world today. This means that worship is likely to become not simpler but rather more difficult and confused. Men today are not looking for simple words. They are suspicious of them. They smack too much of advertising techniques and political slogans. They look for words that express their hopes and fears and unformulated certainties. These are the stuff of our thinking about God and of our attitudes in worship. The prophets of the Old Testament had no simple word to speak. Paul did not go in to the Roman world with an uncomplicated message. The layman's contribution to theology and worship is not to make them simple, however much his protest against the archaic language and obscurantist thinking of our traditional theology and forms of worship may appear to be just that. The layman has to bring into the worship of tomorrow the urgency and confusion of his life in the world today and his intention with other

Christians to take responsible action in it. If he is not expressing his faith there, worship will remain only of relevance (and of rapidly decreasing relevance) to his private life.

This means that ways have to be found to bring the secular world into worship. The opening of such ways at present generally depends on the clergy. And many are increasingly aware of the need. Where clergy are making experiments in worship lay men and women should do all they can to support them and to press them further. It is good when the laity bring to the preparation of worship their suggestions for some topics for intercession and for the sermon. But it is more important that full discussion take place on the issues behind the topics for intercession, and on the problems of today with which the best of sermons can deal only superficially. Full and controversial discussion, reflecting a participation in discussion with others outside the Church, is the main means at present by which the secular world can begin to make contact with the worship of the Church. But such discussion can be merely academic. Indeed the practice of the Church in recent decades has been to keep it academic : to hear all sides, to keep an open mind and never by any means come to a decision to do something. Discussion and dialogue must be combined with a commitment to action; to corporate action and individual action.

Out of such discussion and action new forms and words for worship would inevitably arise, and with them a new sense of corporate commitment and response. The worship of the Church in the last two centuries has concentrated on individual commitment and response. The weakness of our traditional worship is so often that there appears to be nothing else. This has been the beginning and the end of worship. But this question is best left over to the next chapter when we discuss prayer.

5. Prayer and the Laity

Prayer raises almost insuperable difficulties in the minds of many men today. The same is true of worship and the reading of the Bible. We know that from the beginning all these have had their essential place in the life of Christians, and they have been the accepted means of help in the living of the Christian life, but today many people are more aware of the problems they raise than of the help they bring. In so far as prayer is concerned we have to face the intrinsic difficulty of the whole conception of prayer. For us today there are peculiar difficulties arising out of our new knowledge of the material world and of the working of men's minds. But perhaps there is another difficulty which prevents us from even facing such questions. And this is the feeling that lay men and women cannot be expected to have any direct experience of prayer or, for that matter, of worship and Bible reading. These are things that always seem to come to them at second hand from the clergy : things that they are told to do; things that will be good for them; clerical prescriptions for their cure, rather than food that they choose to eat because they like it.

We have no doubt that prayer and worship and the Bible are essential for all Christians and especially for those who are deliberately trying to equip themselves better for their work in the world. But they will only be of value if somehow they have found them out for themselves and have experimented with them, and if they are not just trying to imitate, in a half-convinced kind of way, what the clergy tell them to do.

So in this chapter we want to say something about the

nature of prayer, and something about the peculiar difficulties which prayer has for men and women today. And
then we'll try to be practical in suggesting lines to follow. But here we must be careful, or we may well end
by seeming quite indefinite and unhelpful. For each of us
has to find his own way for himself. In prayer, worship,
and Bible reading we have all suffered too long from instructions. We have to escape from instruction into life.

Prayer is certainly difficult. It pin-points all the pecu-
liarities and difficulties of the standing and the claims of
Christians in the world. It asserts that this is God's
world, and yet it implies that we have to ask him to do
his will. It expresses a peculiar relationship to persons
and things and a conviction that this relationship can
have its effect on them : that we can pray for people and
events in the faith that something will happen. It claims
that we can gain benefits, beyond the rewards and punishments of our actions, in obtaining pardon and peace.
Prayer raises difficult questions even for those who find
its practice satisfying.

For those outside the Church such questions are so
obvious as to lead to doubts about the sanity of those
who pray. They resent the claim that Christians seem to
make when they pray, that they have some special
status in the world, and some power (denied to others) of
achieving private ambitions. They can see no evidence of
this, and if they could they would be furious. But in the
main they are not worried. To them prayer belongs to
the pre-scientific world if not to the world of supersti-
tion.

Yet to the Christian prayer is still something which is
both a natural activity and a duty. It focuses his faith
and his obedience, his failures and his bewilderment. It
brings an immediate quality into the living of his faith. It
demonstrates that his faith is not something he learns
from a book. It is not just a set of doctrines to which he
has subscribed. And, on the other hand, it shows that his

faith is not only a matter of blind obedience. If it were so, there would be some danger of his becoming either self-righteous or despondent. A Christian will lose both humanity and flexibility if there is not another side to his life, open yet hidden, in which he is seeking and finding, knowing and being known. This he finds in prayer.

It is not a thing apart from the rest of his life. It is an essential part of it. It interprets and illuminates his life, sometimes with strange lights. And when we speak of prayer in this way we are not thinking only of that formal practice of prayer, which Christians so often fail to keep, we are thinking also of those moments of illumination which enlighten and sustain us, and without which life would be empty and forms of prayer meaningless. And of this most men and women have some experience. For prayer belongs to all men.

Prayer is like a ladder: the view from each step is different, and as you go up your hold seems to get more precarious. It is this continually changing nature of prayer which makes it so difficult to discuss. A child knows what prayer is. An adult has to learn. It is based on a child's experience, but it has to become an adult activity in which all that a man does is involved. It withers if it remains, as it often does, a memory of childhood.

To a child, to pray is to ask—to ask for something. The dangers of this simple definition are obvious: the dangers of selfishness, of the desire for domination, of getting things without working for them. These dangers are so evident that some would say that prayer has nothing to do with asking for what we want. So it is well for us that Jesus emphatically described prayer as asking. If it were not for this our prayer might well be quite remote from life; an escape into some spiritual sphere. But prayer is not divorced from the ordinary desires of men. It is only natural that whatever seriously concerns us in our lives should rise into our prayers, like bubbles in a boiling pot. It is natural for men to ask and to seek and to knock. There is never any excuse for us to be timid or apologetic in our asking and our seeking and our knocking, even if our questions are embarrassing, our search disturbing, and our knocking only destructive. Our failure is more likely to lie in refraining from asking and being afraid of what we might find and preferring to keep doors closed.

But prayer is not just asking. It is receiving and finding and going through doors. It is an act of response to God and to life. It is the commitment of our wills. It is the expression of our wildest hopes. And it is also our acceptance of a world outside ourselves—the world of other people, the world that was before us and will be here after we have gone. It brings to us an awareness of a purpose beyond our own understanding.

And prayer is not prayer if it is just a man talking to himself. Prayer is thought directed right outside ourselves. It is recognition of a power which makes all life personal. It is therefore in the second person, even though there is something almost terrifying in the idea of talking to God in our own human words. (And it is not any the less so if we address him as 'you' rather than as 'thou'. Indeed the reason why we now use the more customary 'you' is to emphasize the incredible presumption of using words at all.) It is the use of our thoughts and words in a direction outside ourselves but still intensely personal that constitutes prayer.

George Herbert, the seventeenth-century English poet, has some odd and revealing words about prayer. He defines it as 'the heart in pilgrimage ... the Christian plummet sounding heaven and earth ... something understood'. Prayer is, thus, for him the means by which we explore the depths and heights of our experience, by which we gain understanding. This is not merely an intellectual understanding. It is an understanding with our whole being and not just with our minds. But it is understanding; the acceptance of significance.

Prayer is also something we do, to do which we have to discipline and educate ourselves. In this it is like life itself, in that we live and learn to live at the same time. But life that is lived is greater than the learning of it; and prayer is something different from the discipline of prayer. By the discipline of prayer we mean the deliberate attempt to think ourselves into the attitude of prayer, to see ourselves as set in the real world of other people and of all things, to say 'Yes' to this life and the giver of this life. For most of us this deliberate endeavour is necessary, and in doing it we can find help in various ways: in thinking about the actions and words of Jesus and then thinking of our own actions and our experience of life. This is a salutary exercise. Nevertheless, for many people prayer becomes alive not by this regular discipline but because something happens that by its terror or its wonder forces them out of their sceptical detachment from the personal nature of all life.

The moments when ordinary men and women pray naturally and with conviction are the occasions of crisis in their domestic lives. It is easy to sneer at the way in which people turn to the Church for baptism, marriage, and funerals, and have little to do with it at other times. But it is on these occasions of joy and sorrow—at one's marriage or at the birth of a child or at the death of someone dear—that men and women feel the urge to pray and know what they're praying about. This is true also of our public life. When danger threatens or when people are shocked by public grief, then men and women will pray publicly. It is true that we should not need these crises to awake our sensitivity to prayer. The far from ordinary Christian who maintains a constant daily life of vital prayer is one who has somehow learnt to see the life of every day as being just as much a time of crisis or of rejoicing as are the special occasions of domestic and national life. But this is not easy. Indeed, a regular prayer discipline can even produce in those who practise it a kind of obverse insensitivity to ordinary people. Perhaps we need the exceptional to awaken us. Certainly for most men and women it is the dread of the death of a child or the news of the assassination of a president that forces them to their knees.

So in the domestic life of people prayer holds a certain place and meaning. But most men know another world —the world of their daily work. Here prayer seems to hold no place. And this is perhaps the strongest reason why prayer seems unreal to many laymen today.

On the face of it, it must seem strange that prayer should be so remote from a man's work. Often a man's job produces as many occasions of anxiety and crisis as does his family. His work is the commonest cause of his ill-health. The problems, anxieties, frictions, and achievements of his working life may make more demands on him than does his home. His work offers little of the comfort, relaxation, and distraction that his family can provide. And on his work depends his own security for the future and that of his wife and children.

And the world of work is demanding in other ways. It brings a man into constant contact with other men, and these men not of his own choosing. His work, whatever it is, forces him into constant touch with all sorts of people—fellow-workers, employers, employees, customers, clients, patients, pupils. Through his work a man is brought into inevitable contact with his neighbours: not with the selected neighbours with whom he chooses to live, not with the carefully chosen few with whom he is intimate in the club or the golf-course or at church, but with his inescapable neighbours whom he does not choose, and whom he cannot avoid.

Then, just as his work brings him into contact with other people in a widening circle—which now stretches to the ends of the earth—so his work puts him in touch with material things. Work has to do with man's handling of matter. In our work we manipulate, affect, and change material things. When the book of Genesis says that man was made in the image of God and was set in the garden to guard and tend it and has dominion over the earth and everything in it, it is asserting the eternal truth of this. And today man's work raises terrifying questions about his handling of the material world, for he can develop it or destroy it. And this is not a remote fear known only in the studies of scientists; it is obvious to any worker in a naval shipyard or a chemical works.

It is from contact with other men and from the use of material things that, from the beginning of man's history, have come the joys, visions, and achievements that have inspired men, and also the anxieties and frustrations that have divided men. Ultimate questions of justice, co-operation, and purpose have forced themselves on men's attention because of their work. And these questions have arisen not as ultimate questions to be discussed ultimately but as urgent decisions to be taken daily.

Because of these strains, one might expect prayer to be as natural a response to the crises of work as it is to the crises of domestic life. Constant contact with other men, bringing awareness of their needs as well as of their failures and of our inadequate ability to help them; our use of material things, with our doubts as to our misuse of them; questions about the justice of our distribution of the goods we produce; misgivings about the purposes that our work serves: these surely are the very material of prayer.

Yet it does not easily prove so. Prayer is a stranger in the realm of work. It is not that men are unaware of the questions their work raises. They are probably worried by them more acutely than the clergy often think. But it never occurs to them that these questions have anything to do with prayer. And, therefore, prayer has little to do with them.

This is one of the reasons, and perhaps the strongest, why prayer seems pointless to many men today. It is a much more potent reason than any of the intellectual difficulties they may express. Prayer, as they have known it in childhood or in church, seems to have little to do with the gnawing anxieties and wonderful responsibilities of their lives. They cannot see its use. Perhaps it can be used as an escape from insoluble problems, just as activity in the affairs of the local church may be compensation for an inability to do anything effective in the wider world of men. Perhaps it can be seen as a means of maintaining personal standards of behaviour and of concern for others. This is certainly a proper purpose of prayer. But if this is thought by men at work to be the only purpose of prayer, and if prayer fails to have any bearing on the real anxieties of men in their jobs, it will soon seem to them largely a purposeless activity.

If a man faced with a crisis in his work, such as a strike or the loss of his job, is not tempted to pray as he would be when his child is critically ill, he reveals that he does not think of his working life as having anything to do with God's world as obviously his domestic life somehow has. And a divided world is the end of prayer.

Yet the world in which most lay men and women work is coming to be seen more and more as a united world. It is made up of frightening conflicts and tensions between groups and between nations; but these are frightening because men everywhere are at the same time so dependent on each other. In the immediate world of his daily work a layman finds his life made up of demanding relationships which agitate his mind and sustain his life. This is the world of his practical experience. At the same time he is aware that this practical experience is not concerned merely with the surface of things, but through its satisfactions and contradictions leads him into a sense of the abiding meaning of changing events. He senses what Edwin Muir describes as

'... the unseeable
One glory of the everlasting world
Perpetually at work.'

This is the world that the sensitive layman lives in. And if prayer is to mean anything to him, it must be in relation to this world. And if it is to mean anything there, the layman will inevitably want to discover a new significance, and a new magnitude in prayer. And because this is his world and not the world of the clergy he can look to others for advice and some assistance, but he has to do his work for himself.

So prayer for the layman is still often an undiscovered territory which he must penetrate. In this task he will not, unfortunately, receive much help from the conventional teaching of the Church on prayer.

His prayer will be concerned with his whole life and especially with those parts of his life which have not in the past been considered the realm of prayer. He must, therefore, depart from those conceptions of prayer which are appropriate for home and school. He has moved out from the private world of childhood and the directed world of school. He has moved into the public world of work and politics. And the Church in its devotional thinking has not often followed him there.

He will also have to free himself from the language of prayer as he has known it in the Church. The language the Church uses for prayer is usually either the language of a past age or of a man's childhood. As a result the prayers that he has overheard in church have sounded either antiquated or childish and in both cases remote from the life he is living. Prayer means very little if it does not arise out of or speak to immediate experience and immediate needs. A man has to learn that his colloquial meditations may be prayer. He has to learn, not that he never prays, but how often he is praying without knowing it.

In this ecclesiastical ossification of the words of prayer the Bible has had an unfortunate effect. Of course the Bible contains the basic experience which makes prayer real. And inevitably the language of the Bible has influenced the form of the Church's prayers. But in many countries it has been the language of the seventeenth century which with all its majesty and rotundity has moulded the Church's prayer, both liturgical and free, and this has made it difficult for Christians to pray in the simple style of the Gospels.

The effect of the Bible has not been only to make the language of prayer always sound a bit out of date. The Bible deals with daily life but the life it deals with is the life of a pre-scientific, peasant society. It speaks in terms of sowing and reaping, and of simple fighting and fishing. When our life is in terms of engineering and aeronautics, of accountancy and computers, to restrict our prayers to the language of the Bible is to suggest that prayer belongs to an older age and a simpler society and has little to do with modern life.

The task of the responsible Christian in our modern, secular society is to begin to think of the world of his work in the light of his faith, as the men of the Bible did in their vastly different world. This demands both rebellion and perseverance.

And here perhaps is the greatest obstacle. The task is not only difficult: it is painful. Men are reluctant to bring prayer into their daily work, not only because they doubt its effect or because they dread being thought pious, but also because prayer brings awkward questions in its train. For prayer does not make things easier nor does it smooth out difficulties. It raises questions which men would often prefer to leave unasked. It asks nagging questions about personal relationships, about social justice, and about the purpose of our work. It speaks of love and forgiveness. It is easier to use these words freely in a building set apart for worship than in a factory or down a mine or in an office, which on the face of it do not seem to exist to promote forgiveness and love. The reluctance of men to pray may be due to their *honesty*. And this honesty must be preserved. We must be very careful not to use prayer to cover up or as a means of getting our own way, as we sometimes try to do. Our prayer must reinforce our honest questions. We can dare to pray only if we are willing honestly to study the problems of our industrial society. And only so will prayer become relevant and adult.

The education of a Christian in his childhood and youth is to prepare him for his adult life in the responsible world of work and leisure and politics. His continuing education is the means by which he learns to live his life there effectively. And the key to prayer may well lie in his learning the meaning of responsible action. Men know that they have a terrifying responsibility in the world today: they have the power to create or to destroy. They have become as gods, with the destiny of the world in their hands. In these circumstances prayer can seem hypocrisy. Certainly the primitive idea of prayer as beseeching or bribing God becomes futile and blasphemous. But what if this new responsibility is not a case of man usurping God's authority but of fulfilling God's purpose for man in the world? This gives prayer a new direction and a new magnitude. 'Could it be that faith is the joyful acceptance of that responsibility, a refusal to cry to God for help. Faith may mean not more prayer for the coming of God, but more acceptance of responsibility for this world and for our neighbours. . . . It may just be today that it is precisely the man of faith who will not try to use prayer to ask for anything that he can do for himself, but who will stand up to face his neighbour and to accept responsibility for himself and his world and his neighbour.'[1]

1. Joseph Duffey in *Christian Comment*, No. 63, June 1965.

This is true. It sheds a new light on prayer for modern man. Prayer is no escape hatch from the world; indeed true prayer means that we cannot escape from the world and our responsibilities in it. It helps us to see the world, both our immediate world and the wider world of other men everywhere, in its anxieties, hopes, and glory as the creation of God. It should also help us to see our responsibilities, our failures and our possibilities as human beings, both individually and corporately. It's only when we begin to worry a bit more honestly about the world and about ourselves that we'll begin to pray: for then we'll begin to want to.

But we'll have to find out how.

Perhaps our greatest difficulty about prayer is that we think too much about it. We're apt to have such lofty ideas about what prayer should be that we think that it's not for us. Or we think that it raises so many deep theological questions which must be answered before we can begin. And, indeed, these questions will never be answered, if by that we mean that we'll never ask them again. In fact some of these questions are of the very nature of prayer. It is prayer that raises them. The questions we *should* be asking are quite different ones—about ourselves and the world.

Most books about prayer don't help us much today. Indeed they rather hinder. Some of them give us an idea of prayer that is neither intelligible nor attractive. They use technical and theological words that put us off. They are usually based on the experience of men and women who as members of a religious order have devoted themselves to a life of prayer rather detached from personal responsibilities in the world. This is not to question the value of their discipline of prayer for themselves and for the Church. It is based on the life of a committed religious community, and has to overcome many difficulties such as isolation from the world and the monotony of a patterned daily life. These are real difficulties for them, but they are not the difficulties of a layman in the world today. His difficulties arise from his ambiguous involvement with other people in the ever-changing and uncertain nature of his daily life. It is disastrous to ask him to imitate, at remote second hand, the devotional practices of an utterly different kind of life. This is one of the reasons why many loyal church members feel that prayer is not for them, and why so many little books of devotion put people off prayer.

In prayer we must always begin with ourselves in our own situation.

This means beginning with a kind of prayer which is most natural for us. Most of us have our moments when we may not be thinking about God at all but are somehow taken out of ourselves and pause to look at the world, at other people, and even at ourselves in wonder, joy, or terror. These are moments that are necessary for the growth of any child and the health of any grown man or woman. We are lifted up at the sight of beauty. We are taken out of our preoccupation with ourselves by the love of another person. We are ashamed at a true sight of ourselves. Such are moments of essential prayer. It is rudimentary prayer; but it is prayer. Without it we are not likely to develop a more adequate life of prayer. Jesus assumed this kind of natural prayer. He never condemned it. Instead he said two things about it.

First, he said that men should ask and go on asking. They should be like the widow who pesters her neighbour until she gives in. We'll never pray unless we have desires and believe that they should be met. These desires may be quite selfish but unless we are sufficiently alive to want things we'll never even begin to pray.

Secondly, he said that we should pray in secret and not to be seen of men. Obviously he meant that we should not boast about our prayer-life. Probably he meant also that we should not always be discussing it and that we should never assume that others don't pray.

It is with this simple, natural, and sometimes quite selfish prayer that most of us have to begin. But we dare not stop there.

There comes a time, earlier than we often think, when a young man or woman says: 'This is no good. Unless prayer means something more than this, I give it up.' This happens when he begins to face the problems of life in the world today. It probably happens at school when he realizes that soon he will be out in the world. It certainly happens when he gets involved in a job. The simple, natural, and often selfish kind of prayer that he has known (and perhaps learnt mostly in church) no longer meets his case. And he doesn't know how to pray any other way.

The disciples of Jesus were in the same position. They had been taught to pray in childhood, and they probably went on praying as they had been taught until they joined Jesus. Then they found that they were not praying satisfactorily, they had to ask him to teach them to pray. And even then Jesus did not give them very much help. They had to learn other things first. They had to learn to live with him and with each other. They had to face new questions, about their attitude to and treatment of other people, and about all the moral platitudes they had taken for granted. And the only advice that Jesus really gave them about the devotional life was to go on living.

When we try to move into a more adult life of prayer it's not new techniques we need so much as a greater concern about the world in which we live and our way of living in it.

When we begin to do this we'll certainly need some new pattern of prayer. But it will be our own and not one evolved in a monastery. A pattern demands times and places, but we should not be too much concerned about them. We should not be too upset if they fail us or we forget them. More important is to find the fellowship of some like-minded people.

What is essential is a serious concern about ourselves, our way of life, our use of time and money. And a concern about our neighbours, near and far, their needs and our need of them. Unless there is this serious asking, seeking, knocking, there can be no effective prayer, nor can we be putting ourselves in the way of getting an answer to our prayers.

But as well as a serious concern about the world, prayer is an exercise in the abiding virtues of faith, hope, and love.

The faith of prayer is the faith of which the New Testament speaks: not the acceptance of a statement of belief but an acceptance of the reality of life, of the world, of God.

Hope in Paul's list is second only to love. It is not a mood. It is not hopefulness. In the words of Robert Oppenheimer, the American physicist: 'Hope is part of our life, and, thus, part of our duty.' Hope is commitment to the things that must be. It is throwing ourselves into God's purpose for the world. Like faith and love it is an active virtue. The words of prayer are in the language of hope.

And in prayer we confess our obedience to Jesus' command to love one another. Jesus gave his new commandment at the end of his life, after he had taught his men to know each other and other people, and after they had learned to obey his earlier commands—to follow him, to forgive, to go out, to heal. Prayer is our acceptance of this most difficult command. It is our acknowledgement that it knows no limits. It is the confession of our failure and the pledge of our obedience.

There is one question which people ask but which we have not mentioned: 'Does prayer work? Are our prayers answered?'

These are natural questions but they are really off the point. They rest on the idea, still strong in the minds of young people (and one of the reasons why they reject prayer) that it is a kind of shopping list, a pleading for presents from an indulgent but rather forgetful father. We pray because we want things. But our praying does not depend on our getting what we want, any more than our faith and hope and love do. Prayer is part of our life and, therefore, part of our duty.

6. The Bible Is for Adults

There are no examinations and no pass marks in the Christian life. And, therefore, there are no grades of Christians. In particular there is no essential division into intellectual and simple Christians. Christianity is a life. And Christian education is for life.

But this does not mean that a Christian is not called upon to think. An educated young Christian may not get out of loving God with his whole mind by arguing that an illiterate peasant can be a better Christian than he is. This is true. But he himself is not an illiterate peasant. He is an educated citizen of an industrialized nation, and it is as such that he is called to live and think.

It is in this matter of thinking that the Christian of today has probably failed most. The weakest part of his education into the Christian faith has been on the thinking, questioning, intellectual side. This has had serious consequences when his general education has developed this intellectual side strongly in other fields. It is fear of thinking that, more than anything else, has made so many church people frozen in inaction, afraid of change, tied to convention, suspicious of questions, shocked by criticism. The true people of God are those who are as prepared to think with honesty as they are to act with enthusiasm.

The faith of a Christian rests on a few fundamental beliefs to which he is committed. He may have strong opinions on a lot of other things, and indeed he is often prepared to argue at great length about them. But these are not the things for which he would be prepared to die. The beliefs for which he would be prepared to die are probably quite few. On these he will often be inarticulate. And on these he will be continually asking himself questions.

The fundamental beliefs of an educated Christian man are not different from the unconscious assumptions that a child makes from birth—the assumptions that the world can be trusted, that life has a purpose, and that he has a place in this purpose. These fundamental beliefs can never be superseded. They can be shaken. They can be developed. They remain the basic beliefs on which life is lived. They are real to a child, even if he cannot understand them. For the adult they have to develop into an understanding of the world and an acceptance of his particular place in it. It is this that makes an endless demand on our thinking. Because of this Jesus called on his disciples to love God with their minds as well as with their hearts. It is not a matter of seeking ultimate answers: it is doubtful if there are any for us in this life. It is a matter of accepting life in order to live it. The living of life is what concerns man, not the finding of an ultimate answer. Or, if you like it better, the ultimate answer is to be found in the living of life now.

It is to this questioning understanding of life that the adult Christian is called. This is the purpose of his education. This is why his education never ends. Towards the end of his life Paul said that he did not count himself as having comprehended. ('I do not reckon myself to have got hold of it yet.' Philippians 13:13—N.E.B.) In the same way we should never expect to be able to say: 'Now I understand everything fully.'

The trouble with most of us today is that we have not been encouraged to ask questions about our faith. We have been made to feel that it is wrong to do so. We should take note of what Dr Ernest Bruder of the St Elizabeth Hospital, Washington, DC, said on Iona in June 1967: 'The unexamined faith cannot be lived: it can only be pretended.'

Nevertheless, when young people today hear the words 'God' or 'faith' or 'religion' many of them fear that they are being called back to a childish acceptance of unquestioned beliefs. To a few this feeling that they may return to childhood may appeal : they may be glad to believe that it is right to ask no questions. But for most such a retreat will seem quite impossible today. Such childish ideas cannot, as they see it, be fitted into the facts of their daily working lives. If parents and teachers give the impression that they discourage candid thinking about Christian beliefs, the result for the future will be tragic.

This call to think is intimidating, and the average Christian is often appalled by the thinking he is called to do. He is called to think hard and strenuously about our urban and industrial life, about our scientific knowledge of the universe, about the international organization of the world, about war and peace and hunger. And we have got to think about all these things if we are to think about God today.

And when we begin to think about God one of our greatest difficulties is the Bible. The Bible raises for us today serious difficulties which cannot be avoided when we discuss the meaning of the faith and the education of a Christian man. Of these difficulties we can mention four. The first and fundamental problem for us is that the Bible deals with the most difficult topics and problems that men can discuss : the purpose of the world, the meaning of life and death, the destiny of men and of the universe. This is not a question of language at all. It's not the words we don't understand that puzzle us most, but those we do. No words are much simpler than 'In the beginning God', or 'Love your enemies'. But none are perhaps more difficult to accept. The words that have roused men have been easy to understand but difficult to accept. The books that have affected the lives of men and changed the direction of world history have always been controversial.

The Bible will always be a stiff book to read. Modern translations and all the aids of modern scholarship will never make it simple. All they can do is to make us see the real difficulties more closely. The danger is that we simplify the questions it asks.

The second and more obvious difficulty is that the Bible was written long ago and far away—in the Near East, two or three thousand years ago. It is expressed in thought-forms very different from ours today. It is pre-scientific. Its picture of the world is indeed based on the best knowledge available to its writers at the time. But it is not our picture of the world. Of course we have always to remember that it is not only the Bible that is written in pre-scientific language. The same is true of Confucius and the great religious teachers of the East, of Plato and Aristotle and the Greek dramatists, of Shakespeare and Milton and most of our poets. Their views of human life differ greatly the one from the other, but they are united in being pre-scientific. There is a gulf between our modern scientific knowledge of the physical world, and the picture of the universe created by the imagination of the artists, philosophers, and theologians of the past. (And the trouble is that our own imaginations are more affected by the latter than we often think. For this reason we find it almost impossible to form in our imaginations a picture of the world revealed to us by science.) We are moved by Shakespeare and even by Buddha but we know that their views of the physical world were all wrong. Our attitude to the Bible is the same.

In the third place considerable difficulty is caused by the literary forms of the Bible itself. It is difficult for us to read a book the writing of which stretched over hundreds of years, which is written in several languages and which contains opinions in one section contradicted in another. The Bible has not the unity of the *Analects* of Confucius or the *Republic* of Plato, or Shakespeare's *Hamlet*. This is one of its constant difficulties. We find it hard to believe that a book written in so strange a way so long ago has anything to say of moment to us today. It certainly cannot be understood properly without some literary and historical study.

And, lastly, it has been made more difficult for us in that somehow we have come to think that we don't need to study it carefully because we know what it's saying. Most people in this country seem ready to state quite categorically 'what the Bible says'. This is true whether they are using its authority to back their opinions, or whether they ridicule it for the absurdity of its statements. In fact the heterogeneous nature of the Bible is such that we should never say 'the Bible says' but only 'Jesus says' or 'Paul says' or 'Isaiah says'.

These are some of the difficulties in the way of our reading the Bible today. They are very great. We should not try to minimize them; for these difficulties should act as incentive to our thinking. They should prevent us from being content with easy answers. For instance the variety of writers and speakers in the Bible and the frequent contradiction of their words should inspire us to try to assess their authority and to understand their opinions. These difficulties should prevent us from using the Bible as a weapon with which to silence opponents or as unquestionable support for our opinions. They should make us content to use it as a means of examining our own opinions and actions.

What is of first importance is the unity that binds the Bible—Old Testament and New Testament—together. This unity is of three strands, which are not easily disentangled.

The first strand is the importance of the physical world. Today we can argue where God is. We do so because we cannot see him in the material world. We try to find somewhere to place him—out beyond our knowledge of the material world or inside ourselves where the outside world cannot penetrate. And we're worried because we doubt whether either place exists in our imagination or our ignorance.

The Bible starts with quite a different view—that God can never be known to us except through his creation, and that of this material creation man is not something separate but an intrinsic part. We can only know of the existence of God in the same way as we know of the existence of the world or of our own existence. It is an act of faith. But the Bible goes further. It asserts that the world and all that it contains is neither evil nor unreal, as the great religions of the East would suggest. It exists and is good.

This belief in the basic goodness of the world is a terrifying belief. It is much easier to divide the things of the earth into those that are good and those that are bad. It is terrifying to believe that nothing exists or happens that is of no significance. Yet without this faith there can be no serious knowledge. Science is based on the belief that every fact is of significance and cannot be disregarded. A good deal of our lives is spent trying to deny or disregard facts. The first strand of the Bible's unity is its insistence on the reality of all material things and the validity of all facts.

The second strand is belief in purpose. Purpose is implied in the word 'good', as in the refrain that runs through the poem of creation in the first chapter of Genesis—'and God saw that it was good'. A thing is good when it is good for something. Goodness implies purpose, and with purpose we depart from the world of scientific proof and enter life. Today we try to understand things by looking at the past, by finding the cause that has produced the effect, by going back to origins. This is as true of archaeology as of chemistry, of history as of biology. Last century the debate between science and religion was on the question of origins: between Darwin's *The Origin of Species* and what the Bible said about what happened in the beginning. It was the wrong battlefield. When Genesis said 'In the beginning God created', it was not talking about when the world began, but about God as the base and origin of all creation *now*. The Bible does not explain things by origin but by purpose. This is, of course, how we explain our own daily activities. I go into town not because I began to travel in that direction, but because I want to go into the bank. It is my purpose that explains my action. If my actions reveal no purpose, I am regarded as in need of care and protection. Life can be expressed only in terms of purpose—and therefore life escapes measurement and definition.

This makes the Bible a difficult book for us when we compare it with works of modern history and science. It uses different terms. It sees life and the things that happen in life as explained by what is going to happen and not by what has already happened. Abraham goes out to seek a city and never finds it; but his life is to be explained by the nation that came to be. Joseph suffers the cruelty of his brothers, exile, and slavery; but through it all unknowingly he is ensuring the future of his tribe. Moses leads his people from slavery to find the promised land. The exiles pined for restoration. The prophets looked to a new world. The word of Jesus is for the future. His prayer is 'Thy kingdom come'. The Bible ends with the prayer 'Come, Lord Jesus'.

The word 'end' has for us the knell of destruction and negation. 'The end of all things is at hand'—such words are to us words of doom. In the Bible they are a shout of hope. For the end is the goal, the consummation, the fulfilment of purpose.

Perhaps one of the reasons why we have made the Bible so much a book of private devotion is that it is only in the sphere of our private lives that we can dare to speak about purpose and ends. We know that our private actions must be governed by purposes. Our judgement of people's actions is based on our assessment of their motives and aims. And the Bible is an undoubted help to us in this. But the Bible is far less concerned with our private actions than with our public actions. The Old Testament has more to say to the nation than to the individual. The New Testament is about the life of the new humanity. We have come to think that it is futile to judge national actions by ultimate purposes. So the Bible seems naïve to us; and our public life is amoral.

The third strand that runs through the whole Bible is the conviction that the present and ultimate purpose of creation is to be expressed in human terms. Probably one of the reasons why we are afraid of ultimate purpose in national and political affairs arises from our bitter experiences of men's manipulation of public purposes for their own ends. We know that public purposes can be evil. We see no way of controlling them as we know ways of controlling the evil purposes of individual men. So we tend to define any ultimate purpose in life in terms of vague general ends like 'the glory of God' or particular personal ends like 'the good life'. The Bible puts the purposes of creation in almost crudely human terms, and it defines the glory of God in the form of a man. The purpose of God is seen at the beginning in the creation of man 'in his own image'. His final purpose is in the coming of Jesus Christ.

The supreme action of God in Jesus Christ is not an isolated event which gains its pre-eminence by having nothing in comparison before or since. It is foreshadowed in man's earlier history and gives meaning to all men's striving since. The ultimate meaning of life and therefore the final basis of judgement must be in human terms.

The importance of the material world, the conviction

of purpose and the fulfilment of this purpose in human terms are the three strands that make up the cord that ties together the different and differing parts of the Bible and gives it its unity. These three strands represent universal needs in men. These, in their most elementary forms, are the three basic needs of a child—trust in the material world around him, the security of knowing his place in the family into which he is born, and the sense of there being a purpose for him in life which is the incentive that enables him to grow up. The education which he undergoes is for the development of these instinctive feelings into a conscious but questioning acceptance of the world, a conviction (which sometimes makes him despair but brings him back to hope) that this life has a purpose more glorious than his experience warrants and which he must serve.

What the Bible does for a Christian is to hold before him the experience of men who held to these convictions and found them true. And, supremely, it enshrines for him the life and person of Jesus as the only way in which such convictions can be understood—in the actual life of a man.

The great value of the Bible for him is not that it answers his questions. His answers can be found only in himself and in the life of the Church. Its great value is that *it keeps him asking all the questions.* There is scarcely a question that man asks which is not asked in the Bible. And, in the end, the certainty of a Christian does not lie in the finality of any answer, but in the unwavering intention of the quest.

So, for the Christian the Bible is not a book which does his thinking for him. Its value is that it holds him to that search for life without which life is pointless. It forces him to think, and it can be a dangerous book in the hands of those who do not wish to think. It is an irritating book to those who want simple answers which raise no other questions. It is satisfying only to those who are willing to commit themselves to the demands of the purpose of which it speaks and to Jesus in whom that purpose finds its full expression.

This means that a Christian is never afraid of any light that scholarship can shed on the Bible. He is freed from any kind of belief in the literal inspiration of the Bible and knows that the parts of the Bible which speak to him with the greatest authority are those which speak to him most clearly of Jesus.

We are today confronted with new questions and opportunities which often seem to challenge or upset our old beliefs. We have to face today the unprecedented power which is available for men to use. We have to face the need and the chance of finding political unity in the world. And, because the nature of our world is so different, we are faced with the shattering of old ways of thinking and speaking about God and with the necessity of finding ways which are both more personal and more universal.

The challenge to God's people is to live and to think.

It seems sensible to end this chapter with some practical suggestions about reading the Bible today. There are a number of short handbooks which can be very useful : we mention one or two in the Bibliography. Here are a few brief hints to be going on with.

1. The first thing we have to do is always to remember the greatness of the topics of which the Bible treats. We are often tempted to come to it with smaller questions than it is really discussing. Or we wish to use it for particular purposes of our own. Men in the past have found the Bible so useful and inspiring in their personal devotional lives that we sometimes think that this was the main purpose for which it was written. But the Bible was not written to be read in private as a devotional book. Nor was it originally intended to be the subject-matter of theological lectures.

2. Some of it was, indeed, written to be used in wor-

ship. Some of the psalms, for example, were written to be sung in the temple in Jerusalem or by pilgrims on their way up to Jerusalem. And Paul asks that his letters be read aloud to Christians gathered in various places. But these represent only a small portion of the Bible.

3. The Bible was written, not to be read, but to be listened to. To people largely illiterate and certainly with few books to read, the spoken word is much more direct and personal than the printed word can ever be for us. It demands the response of obedience or of a question.

4. The Bible is essentially the record of the experience of a people. It has, indeed, many significant things to say about the actions and experiences of individuals. But what it is dealing with from beginning to end is how people have found together a new experience of life and therefore of God. It begins with a tribe and it ends with the new humanity in Christ. And, in between, are all the experiences of men in war and peace, in prosperity and poverty, under oppression and in power. What makes the story significant for all men is that it deals with the common experiences of men with an understanding and vision which are unique.

We cannot therefore understand the Bible or gain any understanding or vision from it if we approach it just as private individuals, withdrawn and isolated from the political world in which we live. It is as members of a group which reflects a variety of practical experience, and which asks many questions, that we are likely to gain most from the study of the Bible.

5. We should always remember that nearly all the events of the Bible take place in the open air. We have shut the Bible very securely within four walls—of church or school or home. Very little of what the Old Testament records takes place within four walls. More of what the New Testament tells took place in a house (but, let us never forget, very seldom in a place of worship). The setting of the Bible is in the wilderness, on the hill-

side, in the market-place, the field, and the street. Perhaps we have to read it out in the world, with the sound of the wind and the sea, with the distraction of the traffic and the noise of men at work, to get the full human, worldly taste of the Bible and begin to understand what it is all about. The Bible is not of use only in the library or in church services. We should think of ways of getting it, as it were, out of doors again—on pilgrimage.

6. Yet, at the same time, we have to remember that the Bible is a collection of books, each written or compiled by one person with a particular theme or purpose which gives it unity. Our practice, which goes back a comparatively short time, of printing the Bible in chapters and verses, destroys this unity; and it makes us think of it as a collection of sayings or mottoes or arguments to quote. We should read any book of the Bible with the respect we give to any other book. We should try to understand what it is saying *as a whole*. We should not be surprised that these different books have different emphases. For example, we are the richer in our knowledge of Jesus from having four Gospels, each with its particular interest.

7. It is useful to remember how these various books are divided up and grouped.

The main division is, of course, between the Old Testament and the New. And perhaps the word 'testament' is rather confusing. It is good to remember that Jesus never referred to the 'Old Testament' but to 'The Law and the Prophets'. The Law and the Prophets are the two main divisions of the Old Testament, with another section, 'The Writings', comprising Psalms, Proverbs, Song of Songs, Ecclesiastes, Esther, and Job.

The Law (Torah), comprising the first five books of the Old Testament (Genesis, Exodus, Leviticus, Numbers, Deuteronomy), means much more than the word 'law' means for us. It means something much wider than the ten commandments. The Law is the record of the whole experience by which the Jews became a people with a unique way of life, expressed in a social and religious code and in a passionate hope. The books of the Law tell how they became this people. They tell of the events of their history: in particular of their escape from slavery in Egypt. They also tell of the laws the people had to keep if they were to remain a people. These laws were fundamentally economic rather than religious. They had to do with the tenure of the land, the sharing of food, the claims of the destitute. The Law meant a way of life. So they could rejoice in the Law.

'The Prophets' are the books of the Old Testament prophets—Isaiah, Jeremiah, Ezekiel, Amos, Joel, Hosea, and the others, including Jonah. They are complementary to the Law. They recall the people to the true meaning of the Law, especially by insisting that the Law is basically economic and that it is worse than useless to keep the religious instructions of the Law and disregard its fundamental economic demands. They also call the people to a new vision of the destiny of the world. They do this in varying ways: by denunciation, by visions, by stories—as in the book of Jonah, in which the prophet makes his hearers appreciate the new and strange idea that God cares for all men by telling a story that held their interest and aroused their questions.

The New Testament is parallel to the Old Testament, with the Gospels in the place of the Law and the Epistles in place of the Prophets. The Gospels tell the events which brought to the world a new way of life and the teaching which governs it. The Epistles show how this way of life works out in the actual situations of men in the decades that followed.

8. We are liable to two temptations in reading the Bible. One is to apply its words literally to our situation. It is always easier to take words literally than to think out what their essential teaching means in our situation.

The other temptation is to decide ourselves what the Bible should be saying before we read it. We can, for instance, disregard the teaching of the Sermon on the Mount by dismissing it as 'mere humanism'! Or we can dismiss Paul's words about the abiding nature of faith, hope, and love, because we have a fundamental bias against his doctrinal teaching.

Our reading of the Bible—especially our corporate study of it—demands two things of us.

One is that we ask what the book or the passage means. This we must do quite fearlessly. But we must do it honestly by using the means at our disposal for understanding the Bible.

The second is equally important. We must also be asking what we should be doing in our own immediate situation today, *and we must be intent not only on asking but on doing.* Otherwise we cannot get any help from the Bible.

Part Two
Laity Education for
Tomorrow's World

7. What Has Gone Wrong?

It may very well be that the Church of Jesus Christ has now achieved some theological understanding of what it is to be a layman in the modern world. There is little doubt that the books published in Europe and in the United States in the last twenty-five years have helped us—in theory—to rediscover the New Testament teachings about the ministry and the priesthood of all believing Christians, whether they be bishops or bellhops, suburban housewives or Pentagon politicians. But now, in the early 1970s, where are the results of all this 'rediscovery of the laity'? Why—especially in the United States—has the cause of laity education gone so sour, and even so dull?

We have had very strong advice that there is no need in North America for any more books on the techniques of adult Christian education. This is clear to anyone who looks at denominational or seminary bookstores; and indeed we can list only a few of the best American titles in the Bibliography. In our British edition we have offered a fairly extensive classification of the different ways in which the education of the laity can be organized and developed. There is no need to do this for United States readers, but we venture to suggest that a summary of this classification will help readers to detect what may have gone wrong in some at least of the American churches, and why many of the high hopes for a lively and informed Christian laity—to be found in the literature of the '50s and early '60s—are now so muted.

If you wish to look at a scheme of laity education anywhere in the world Church—from Ibadan to Edinburgh or Indianapolis, and no matter what denominations are involved—it is helpful to consider the following questions (which we have in fact evolved after a considerable number of consultations and discussions with all kinds of experimental ministries and organizations).

1. What is being learnt together? Perhaps an old-fashioned question, but we put it first, for a good many excellent experiments miss out the awkward topics without noticing this.

A Christian today has responsibilities in six areas of life, and for each of these he must work out a *theology*, a way of looking at them in relation to his faith :

a. His church duties.

b. His personal and family and sexual relationships.

c. His relations with his neighbours—the people around him he can know personally.

d. His job; and, more than this, his involvement (which is quite inevitable if he is not to live in a log cabin—and without a credit card—in the modern economic system which reaches far beyond his personal ken and far beyond the territorial United States).

e. His leisure and his leisure planning and spending. But we mean a *theology of leisure*, not a vague pseudo-puritan condemnation of leisure.

And above all, and particularly above all in the United States, a Christian today must work out his faith in relation to f. politics and the public life.

There must be such an analysis of content, because to avoid the harder questions of industry, economic life, leisure, and politics simply produces flabby Christians.

The other questions to be asked about laity education can be listed very summarily.

2. Who are trying to learn something together? Who has joined in, and who's left out?

3. How long is the learning process taking? A more

important question than it sounds, and we return to it later.

4. What techniques are you using?

5. What staff can you find?

6. Where is this learning to take place?

7. What about finance?

8. What kind of an organization and structure can you have?

Some of these questions we can get out of the way very quickly. There is, as we have indicated, no shortage of American books on techniques in laity education, and we only wish that some of the more stodgy Christian educators in Britain and in Europe would hurry up and read them! We must admit, however, to an uneasy feeling that in the States Christian educators, just like their secular colleagues in the public school systems and universities, tend to fall rather easily for educational 'fads' and fashions, whether they be the playing of 'war games' on expensive computers or the achieving of total non-verbal communication in joyous mud baths. We are not by any means at all suggesting that such experiments are to be forbidden; but there is sometimes a rather hasty—and very expensive—tendency for a diocese or an experimental retreat centre to find a new 'emphasis' which it will pursue feverishly for a year or so, and then drop in favour of another newer-than-new technique. In particular, we do urge that those designing laity education schemes try to offer a fairly wide spectrum of different techniques to suit different people and their needs. In Christian education there is very rarely one 'party line' to which everyone must conform.

We say something more about the question, *Where shall laity education take place?* in later chapters. Probably we need refer very little to the provision of *staff* except for one comment. There is a very strong concealed bias in American laity education—as no doubt elsewhere—to use clergy and a certain type of laity as resource people in laity education. Without wishing at all to criticize, dare we say that they appear to be rather 'churchy' most of the time—even when they are most desperately trying to be 'secular'? This is no doubt quite inevitable, for they are generally employed by, trained by, and instinctively reflect the concerns of church organizations and church seminaries. But in any scheme of laity education their views and ideas need to be balanced and even confronted by the views and ideas of other laymen, whose education and pre-suppositions and career expectations come from *quite different and much more secular backgrounds*. For instance, the views of a professional Christian educator about our daily newspapers, about the policies of a New York City bank, or about the running of a state welfare system must be considered alongside those of lay people employed in such journalism or banking or welfare work, and also together with the considered opinions of other lay people, such as economists and political scientists, who can detect some of the social consequences of such work. It is an elementary point, but we emphasize it; otherwise the dialogues about such matters will simply be phoney.

We hope we shall not cause offence if we now move to certain weaknesses in the American church scene which seem to us very serious and ominous for the future. As British observers we are very aware of the infuriatingly patronizing attitudes of many foreign visitors to the United States; and we are very sensitive to the deep and painful troubles which now beset that great country. But we have to say that it seems to us that the greatest weakness of the laity of the American churches is that they still have not worked out their faith in terms of *economic and industrial life and both national and international politics*. There are apparently thousands of

American Christians who seem to hold a theory of politics appropriate to dutiful slaves in the later Roman Empire. 'The great ones in Washington or New York know best. Our duty is to be loyal to their better judgement (even over Vietnam).' And there are hundreds of thousands of good church people who have a political theory appropriate to the villages of mediaeval Europe, or to the early homesteads and small towns on the prairies. 'Yes, we will see that our little town, our good clean suburb, our vacation village, or our sunset city is run decently. We will pay for our children's schools, and keep our little hospital going, and beautify our corner of America. But don't ask us to bother about the problems of Chicago, or down-town Detroit, or Washington, D.C. And certainly not far off countries like Brazil or Cambodia.'

This is, of course, a very natural human phenomenon: it is very much easier to 'love' or at least to be aware of people of your kind in your street than to worry about justice to the Indonesians or the Outer Mongolians. (And Christian education techniques that concentrate almost entirely on deep personal relationships sometimes unconsciously reinforce this bias: Christians have to work for just and fair non-personal relationships with many people whom they will never know the names of, let alone have sensitivity sessions with.) The world is only just becoming anything like a global unit—economically we have now been interdependent for about a hundred years, politically for about fifty, socially we have hardly begun.

A retreat from world problems is common enough in the comfortable suburbs of southwest London or the small country towns of western Germany. But it does seem to be a special weakness of American church people that they have never worked out the Christian responsibilities of living in a giant twentieth-century democracy —with all its harsh imperfections—of being citizens not only of a suburb but of a metropolitan region, of a state, of a nation, and of a growing world community in which the United States, for good or ill, is the greatest single power. When radicals in the Netherlands in 1968 sent in to *The New York Times* their 'votes' for the American Presidential election, this had no legal force at all. But it did symbolize the responsibilities which the American President and the whole American people have over Britain and Europe and the rest of the world, whether they and we like it or not.

Of course, any involvement of the Christian laity in economic and political affairs has two major and familiar dangers in it. We have known in Europe, and some areas of New England have also experienced, the perils of an institutional church involvement in *party* politics, whether it be a puritan identification of Church and State or a Roman Catholic instruction of the faithful in the right way to vote. But the strong U.S. constitutional doctrine of a separation between Church and State has never meant and can never mean an abdication of the individual Christian's responsibilities as a citizen. It may well be that bishops and other Church leaders need to be extremely careful before they say 'the Church teaches' or 'the Bible teaches' a given line in politics or economics; but a proper caution here has so often led to a very timid and improper reluctance to put such matters on the agenda of Christian discipleship and decision-making.

And here we come to the second and more serious difficulty, which ordinary Christian people in the United States must surely learn to face and not to avoid. Of course laity and laity involvement in political affairs, in civil rights, in racism, in questions of industry and finance and labour, will lead them into acute controversy. And very many Christian people are still afraid of and unskilled in managing controversy. They enjoy a polite discussion, but cannot take a strong argument or a flaming row. (And some of the new radicals know this, and almost enjoy the pain and confusion they can stir up, instead of themselves seeking to use controversy intelligently and profitably.)

This is above all a matter of the true nature of Christian fellowship. It is not sitting on and suppressing your own true opinions because you are afraid you may upset some fellow Christian (an attitude, this, that will kill all true education). Nor is it gloating in harsh confrontation and self-righteously shocking and stunning your opponents. It is speaking the truth, clearly and sharply and in as much love as you can manage, and then listening to the truth in love as the other man sees it. The great achievement of some of the continental lay centres, and of the German *Kirchentag* movement, is that they have achieved some skill in Christian controversy. Perhaps this is especially difficult for American Christians, who are sometimes hung up about being 'loved' and 'appreciated' (particularly if they are well-meaning, white, middle-class conservatives). But controversy and responsible compromise and partial success and conditional loyalties are the ways in which the political and economic life of a great state is maintained, and the ways in which—sometimes—the poor are clothed and the elderly housed and the hungry fed. And, as we argued at some length in *God's Frozen People*, Christian lay people simply have to recognize their involvement in all of this. As Edmund Burke once wrote so wisely, 'For evil to triumph, it is only necessary for good men to do nothing.' Or, to bring it down to contemporary politics, in the words of George Jean Nathan, it may often be that 'bad officers are elected by good men who don't vote'.

Another question which is surprisingly relevant to the present malaise in American laity education is *Who are to learn together?* This is because it seems to us that it is so often answered in a kind of pseudo-democratic way.

'Of course, the laity need some education. We'll have a
course in Lent, and anyone can come.' But the painful
fact is that if a church course or conference is nominally
'open to all : everybody welcome', some people come and
some people are quite determined to stay away.

This may be just a matter of the churchiness of the
group; and we refer to this problem in later chapters
when we consider how likely it is that church educators
will make contact with the kind of laity who sing in the
choir and come to the women's fellowship; and how
such kinds of people may, with the best will in the world,
choke off the 'harder', more secular, perhaps less prissy
laity, who are nevertheless of the first importance in
'being the Church in the world'. Often it is just the plain
fact that a conference or a course for 'all the laity'
generally recruits average laymen of average ability and
competence. It is unattractive for people who are slow
learners and are not used to middle-class habits like
reading pamphlets and organizing discussion groups; and
it will bore to tears the very able and competent.

It must be admitted here that the problems of the
education of blue-collar workers in a century of rapid
and threatening social and economic change are common
to many areas of Europe and America and are part of
the general educational perplexities of our time. The Los
Angeles or the Mississippi school systems are as puzzled
as the churches in dealing with children from workers'
homes, who don't fit in with 'literary' and middle-class
styles of education. We are a little perplexed to find
American Catholic parishes almost as defeated by these
problems as Protestant ones, for they have a very considerable proportion of blue-collar workers in their
membership. (And their votes and social attitudes are
very important in city problems, in opening unions to
blacks, and in offering housing to minority groups; and
they can be bitterly conservative in such matters.) There
are some hints from European Catholic experiences, for

example, with the 'Young Christian Workers' movement in Britain and elsewhere. There have been some promising experiments by Dr Letty Russell in Harlem, New York (see Bibliography). But this is one of the toughest problems facing all educators at the moment: how to devise styles of learning for people who don't take to traditional or even innovative high-school and church learning procedures.

There is an almost equal weakness in provision for the very able. Perhaps it is the latent anti-intellectual bias which is still very strong in American church life (and which can sometimes produce sloppy slogans like 'Don't think: feel!'—as if Christians did not have to learn *both* to feel and to think deeply and strenuously).

Perhaps it is a lingering false idea of human equality which suggests that it is somehow 'wrong' to consider the special needs of the real decision-makers in our society today, who in their secular responsibilities deal daily with wonderfully and excitingly sophisticated ideas and systems, and are then asked to be satisfied with pathetically mediocre Christian education programs. Small wonder that they attend more and more reluctantly on Sunday mornings, and that they have almost given up any hope that the Church can offer them an understanding of the faith deep enough and complex enough to match their secular learning and involvement. They may be asked to help with the church's housekeeping in relatively trivial ways, such as auditing the parish books or advising on the architecture of the new Christian education building. But they are not offered any help in thinking theologically about their enormous responsibilities in investing millions of dollars a day, or hiring and firing thousands of men, or trading overseas. It is very much to the credit of the 'new left' that it has seen and proclaimed the fundamental social and structural responsibilities of such establishment decision-makers (when the churches, too often, have kept silent about foreign trade or inner-city real estate except to be grateful for the dividends). Unfortunately the debate or the mudslinging from the left is often confined to simplistically emotional terms—and this is true of church radicals too. There is, for sure, a deeply disturbing and sharply critical examination to be made of many of the ways in which present economic and political organizations work, both in Europe and in the United States. But this demands much hard thinking, much systematic research, much competent critical analysis, and much understanding of the appalling alternatives with which many decision-makers are faced. For there is simply never enough money to go round; nor would there be if all the wars stopped tomorrow.

We would reinforce this plea for a much more thorough provision of styles of Christian learning for able people with an emphasis on the one question about laity education which is often ignored—*How long?* This is a far more important question than most people think, and most experiences of Christian education for adults are much too short to be really effective.

We suggest that all effective Christian education has four elements in it, which perhaps we may indicate by the following diagram:

INPUT ⟶ ARGUMENT (if you like, 'dialogue')

SUPPORT ⟵ DECISION 'Commitment'
'Conversion'

It is commonplace that one of the great weaknesses of so-called liberal education has been that it deals almost entirely in two of these: *Input* and *Argument*. You hear a challenging speech, you have small discussion groups, you engage in what has been called 'uncommitted dialogue'. And then you go home until next week or next month when you 'do' the United Nations as your next topic. The ineffectiveness of much of this kind of education was well illustrated recently by the Dutch *Sjaloom* leader Dr Edward van Hengel when he commented, 'Probably discussion without decision in our day is not only a waste of time, but also *sin*'.

And so, many Christian educators have returned, with an almost evangelical fervour, to an emphasis on decision-making, on altering your life-style and your political position in response to the input you have heard and the argument you have joined in. 'Not to decide is to decide,' insists Harvey Cox, and there has been a most welcome reaction against spiritual sitting on the fence, even if sometimes there is a demand for an instant response to a decidedly unclear (even if shouted) challenge.

But there it stops. Just as the Billy Sunday or Billy Graham campaigns so often raised you to an ecstatic peak of deciding for Christ, and then afterwards there was a personal and emotional let-down which left you floundering in self-doubt and loneliness until the next revival campaign, so even the most challenging Christian education procedures today often forget the fourth element in Christian learning—*the support structure that will help you maintain and develop your commitment to a new involvement and way of life*. The proper name for this would be Christian fellowship; but unfortunately the word has been so often corrupted to mean not the mutual support of Christians dedicated to new ways of life and witness but the cosy companionship of those determined to oppose change in the Church and to defend out-moded ways of life and witness. How many excellent new kinds of fellowship groups, founded fifty years ago, are now bastions of old-fashioned church life! And how quickly even the newest radical church groups can decay in the same way if they fall to the temptations of intellectual and spiritual pride and say, 'Well, at last we have the truth of the Gospel for the 1970s', instead of insisting; 'Our fellowship must have self-criticism built into it. We must constantly ask for new input, more argument, and further decisions to fit the challenges of the days ahead. Or we shall fossilize too!'

Sometimes a local parish can provide such an innovative, critical, constantly learning group for its lively laity. Sometimes it can't because the needs of such laity may be too complicated and specialized and too radical for a parish and its minister to cope with. And here there are important questions of *structure*, which we can consider only briefly here. It is taking the Church as a whole a very long time to learn that in the future its structures are bound to be multiple and plural in form, and that the old hopes of one neat, tidy organization are gone for good. In the future some church organizations will be ecumenical—more, we hope—but some will probably stay denominational. Some will be local and parochial, others will be regional and national. And the same is true in laity education. It is very likely that if a group of housewives want to talk about, for instance, sex education for their small children, they can be given the chance to do this locally—hopefully with two or three local women's groups joining together ecumenically. But if a parish has a bright young Christian journalist or lawyer in its congregation, it is very unlikely that he can find an adequate kind of education and support there. He needs the chance to join with other journalists or lawyers from his metropolitan area, or even elsewhere in the country. And a wise minister will know this and seek out opportunities for him to do this, and not try to keep him in a narrow and frustrating loyalty to his local church.

We have left to the end the plain reason why, so far as we can see, many of the laity of the American churches have not been properly equipped for their work of ministry, and why so many of them now face the present time of crisis pitifully untrained and ill-educated. It is not a shortage of ideas, nor a weakness in theological analysis of the role of the laity today and tomorrow. It is a simple refusal to face the questions of *finance*. It is an appalling shortage of staff and money for laity education because it comes low in the list of church priorities.

And this is rather odd, in the United States of all places, and in American churches, which are by European standards wonderfully well financed (yes, even in the present difficult days). But it is true. Again and again we have noticed church leaders—Catholic cardinals and Presbyterian moderators and the rest—give a fine and even impassioned verbal tribute to the essential role of the laity in the Church of tomorrow, and the value of laity education, and so on. But when you look at church budgets you see the true story. There was one major denomination which had a grandly named department for experimental laity education—or something of the kind—and its programme budget (for the whole continental United States) was eventually reduced to some two thousand dollars a year. There was another giant organization which could hardly find five hundred dollars a year to examine how its expensive policies affected the laity. There is, so far as we can discover, no seminary anywhere in the entire United States which as yet has found the money for an adequate, and adequately kept up-to-date, library collection on the work and education of the laity throughout the world. (The Audenshaw Foundation is trying now to inspire two or three seminaries to do this; but progress has been very slow—because of the same kind of budget difficulties). Indeed, as we have learnt through several years of painful experience, laity education suffers from a kind of sentimental 'tokenism' in the major American churches. Like motherhood, you can't be against it; but there are far more important things to worry about.

Such shortsightedness has brought its own rewards. The so-called 'laity backlash' which many church leaders have experienced in the last two or three years is nothing more than they should have expected. In the modern world, whether you are a Catholic or an Episcopalian or a Methodist bishop, you cannot expect any longer to have a docile laity—'good church people' who will faithfully follow your lead from the pulpit, whether it is to build parochial schools or to give money to the inner cities. As we have pointed out in our introduction, you have two alternatives. You will either have an increasingly sullen, apathetic, absent, and ignorant laity or you will have to risk a good deal of money and try to produce a critical but critically *educated* laity. The chances of the last twenty-five years have largely been wasted, and now we feel very much afraid that the American churches, in particular, do not have much more time in which to make up their minds on this matter.

8. Laity Education at the Local Level

In the difficult process of becoming responsible citizens in the modern world, the place that determines our progress is almost certainly just where we are—in our homes, with our neighbours, at our work, and in our local church. If we are serious about what we are doing as Christians, we cannot indeed stay there all the time. We need to make enquiring contact with the wider world. If we are wise, we'll make use of some of the centres and projects mentioned in the next few chapters. But unless our Christian education is affecting us where we are and live, it will not matter much how many outside courses we attend. For what we do at home, and with our neighbours, and at our work (which is still, even in these days, often local), and in our local church very often decides what kind of life we live in country, church, and world.

Christians concerned with the development and growth of the laity tend to swing between the use of the word 'education' and the word 'training'. Each has its difficulties. Training suggests a vigorous course of instruction and practice for the doing of something well, be it swimming a hundred yards or learning to be a plumber. Education, for many people, is still associated rather with school and college. It is something that happens to or is imposed on you, especially when you are young. We have used the phrase adult Christian education; but, especially at the local level, it must be something rather different from either formal education or training. It is essentially informal. It is not based on external authority or discipline. It depends solely on the

pleasure we receive or the interest it arouses or our sense
of responsibility. In other words it depends on whether
we are lively people and on whether it appeals to lively
people. It has to be immediate in its appeal, with an eye
to the future but even more alive to the present. In fact
it has to do with the way we live our lives or the way
we want to live our lives, or our attempts to find a new
kind of life which we can live for its own sake or, in
other words, to the glory of God. This style of lively and
informal laity education must be worked out at the local
level in four areas: in a man's home, with his neighbours, at his work, and in his local church.

In the home. This kind of education is most influential
where it is most informal, and that is in the home or
wherever it is that a man looks at TV and glances at the
papers and talks and argues and sometimes reads; when
a man is at leisure, and does things just because he wants
to do them—and is free to do nothing at all. Of course
we remember that, when we were children, home was
not always the place where we did what we wanted.
Perhaps we think of it as the place where we were told
to do things. We now see it as the place where we were
being trained, and where we acquired tastes and standards which now we cannot quite get rid of even if we
want to. We like to think that we are giving the same
kind of training to our children.

Perhaps we don't realize that the most influential
things in our life at home as children were not the pro-
hibitions and commands but quite different things, not
the formal words of instruction but the words we overheard when our parents did not think we were listening,
and the grown-up talk that revealed what they were
really interested in. In our turn we don't always realize
how determining and educational for our children is our
attitude to our neighbours and our way of speaking
about them, our detachment from, or our involvement

in, the life around us, and the opinions we express when we do not think we are being overheard. Certainly we don't sufficiently realize how we are *still educating our- selves*, for good or ill, by the way we live at home. For so often our life at home determines our public life.

In the last century, at the head of the worthwhile activities at home would have been the reading of books. Books were regarded as the main, if not the only, tools of adult education. According to some critics TV has taken the place of reading and has destroyed the life of the home. It is very doubtful if this is true. It is certainly impossible to assess the amounts of reading done in the home then and now and to compare them. All that we can say with certainty is that there is an ever-increasing demand for books in Britain; that more books are pub- lished every year; that more books are borrowed from libraries each year. Are they read? No one can say to what extent. But one can certainly say that the travel- ling public is a reading public. Even in buses people try to read newspapers and books.

Watching television is certainly a time-absorbing activity which may sometimes take priority over read- ing, but which often leads to people reading. Cynical remarks are often made about people whose eyes are glued to the TV screen. We forget that similar remarks used to be made about the reading of trivial novels. Why it should be regarded today as worse to have your eyes glued to the screen than to the printed page it is difficult to say. It is perhaps because reading demands more application and effort and perseverance, and is therefore more praiseworthy. But do you not have to concentrate more in watching the screen? You have to remember what you have viewed. With a book you can turn back the pages if you have forgotten. And reading is a solitary business. Television offers the possibility of corporate experience and discussion.

In both reading and television there is an element of

choice. With TV it is limited and controlled. With books it is almost limitless, and there is certainly more trash published and avidly read than is ever shown on the screen. We have thought it right to provide people with a limitless choice through libraries and cheap books. We are faced with an utterly different problem with television. It is probably the greatest instrument of education that man has ever devised. How do we develop and control it for the greatest good of men? This is a problem for us as political citizens. A great deal depends on how we learn to use it in the free atmosphere of our homes.

But just as with books, we cannot treat TV programmes as all of a kind. They can be roughly divided into three categories: information, entertainment, and education. Clearly they merge into each other. And equally clearly no programme will educate unless at the same time it entertains. But these three are distinct and legitimate uses of television. They should be used and judged in different ways. These distinctions apply also to radio. What other people read does not directly affect us. What other people want to view may limit and affect our viewing. For most families there has to be a concensus on programmes; and majority appeal over the nation will mainly determine what choice is available. The kind of entertainment people want differs with age and tastes. We have to be careful not to be superior about other people's choice of entertainment. It may indeed be one of our ways of getting to know them. And what instructs us may be boring to others. In our own use of TV and radio we should welcome what increases our knowledge or stretches our imagination, what makes us ask questions and at the same time be understanding of the different interests and needs of very varied groups of other people.

But the great danger of any use that we make of television is that we become merely spectators. (We don't escape from this danger by remembering that it applies also to going to church.) The danger is not in our learning by looking, for we can often learn more by seeing a picture than by reading or hearing. The danger lies in the acquisition of a spectator's attitude as the proper one for life. The political interviewer on TV is much more obviously a detached observer of the political scene than is the anonymous writer of a leading article in a newspaper. We see him from his superior detachment questioning and trying to catch out men with heavy responsibilities in the life of the nation and of the world. This attitude can easily be transferred to the viewer, and can induce in him a cynicism on matters in which he in the end has a responsibility.

It is noticeable that this cynically detached attitude of the political interviewer is quite different from that of the interviewer in matters of art and science. Here the interviewer tries to draw out with sympathy and understanding the peculiar and often obscure ideas of the artist or the scientist. Television has certainly extended for a great number of people their knowledge of music and the pictorial arts. It has also given to many some kind of understanding of modern science. It has also, and more importantly, made people aware of how other people live in different parts of the world and has removed the cloak of superhuman greatness from the leaders of the nations and revealed them as ordinary men. But it can hardly be said that we have learned to use TV to educate ourselves in our understanding of the *political* problems of our contemporary world. It has certainly not helped us towards responsible participation. We are so often left with the impression that the really superior person is the interviewer, and that his qualifications are a certain moral aloofness and an intimate knowledge of other people's failings. It may be that television cannot do anything itself about this without appearing to indulge in obvious forms of political pro-

paganda. The answer is probably to be found in the re-
actions and discussions of informal audiences, who alone
can produce a spur to action and involvement. This
ought to affect the style of political discussion on the
air.

The planned Open University may be able to help here.
The use of television in higher education will depend
on the development of new forms of discussion between
viewer and viewed. It is also potentially important as a
way of experiment in the use of TV in all informal adult
education. It should also assist people in their homes to
learn to use the ordinary TV programmes for informal
discussion. Indeed it may well be that TV offers far
greater opportunity for general adult education than did
the private reading or the public lectures of the past; and
it is excellent that the British churches are now actively
sponsoring the formation of TV viewing groups who will
develop a style of carefully and sympathetically watching not just religious programmes but other serious BBC
and ITV productions. And the greatest value of television
lies where its critics seem most to sense danger—in the
fact that its programmes go out to all indiscriminately,
that audiences cannot be selected and that everyone is
free to make his or her own response. This common
educational potential of TV explains perhaps why the
Republic of South Africa refuses to have it.

The home can become a most influential means of
adult Christian education, if it is the place of discussion
of those issues that TV brings into it. Generally it provides something of a built-in clash of opinion between
the generations; and this is invaluable.

But means have to be found to encourage the ability
to express opinions and to be more articulate. It may be
suggested that the supposed decrease in reading and its
displacement by television is much less important than
the decrease in the habit of *writing*. A taxi-driver in New
York, when asked by a recent visitor what was now the

postage for local mail, replied 'I don't know. I once wrote a letter but that was six years ago.' The telephone has taken the place of the letter for many people. 'Phoning and the use of mechanical means of dictation do not lead to concise expression. They tend to verbosity or repetition, and the labour of writing or typing is perhaps necessary to train a person in logical brevity. The writing of letters played an important part in the adult education of our forefathers and was a step towards public speaking and political action. One of the things that a man should do who wishes to be a responsible citizen is to develop some freedom in writing.

But whatever are the activities that go on at home— TV, reading, writing letters, gossip—they are invaluable means of education because they are informal, and involve other people.

With his neighbours. A man does not spend all his leisure time at home. He goes out among his neighbours to participate in some kind of activity. He plays golf. He talks to his neighbour over his hedge. He drinks beer in a pub. He runs a Scout troop. He attends a meeting. He goes to church. He canvasses in a by-election. He goes to a football match. No one man engages in all these activities, but most men and women do something of their own choice with their neighbours. And the things they do with their neighbours, be it only talking in the bus, strongly influence their opinions and their actions. The company of his neighbours is where a man tests his reaction to what he sees on TV or reads in the papers or discusses with his family. The development of communication through mass media has brought into a woman's discussion and concern a much wider area of common knowledge and interest than in the past. Then the newspapers catered for different classes and amusements were divided socially, as, for instance, in the difference between the theatre and the music hall. Now you can assume that millions have seen the same interview or heard the same music or watched the same game.

It is the sharing of the same pleasures or the same interests or the same responsibilities that leads a man into doing things with his neighbours. We can deepen our pleasures and widen our interests and grow in responsibility by a more discriminating choice of the things we do, and—and this is as important—by a greater intention that our association with our neighbours be based at least sometimes on serious concerns and not in trivial common interests. The health of a democratic society depends on the vitality of its informal groups to develop a responsible public opinion and to educate its members in participating in public life. And much of this is done, quite informally, in people's leisure life with their neighbours.

In his job. Thirdly, in the unavoidable and informal education of a man there is his job. Sometimes, especially in a great metropolis, he will leave his locality for his work, and then he may need some of the supplementary kinds of Christian education which we mention in later chapters, and which his local church cannot provide for him. But whether he travels one mile or twenty to his work the job itself is, after his home, the most powerful factor in his adult education. For in it he is anything but a spectator. In it he cannot choose what he will do and what he will not do. It is the only part of his education which has a formal side: in very many kinds of occupations today a man has to undergo some sort of technical training, resulting in some kind of qualification. There are of course those who are quite unskilled, but for many people technical training is going to become more demanding in time and more rewarding in efficiency. We should not think that because it is enforced and utilitarian it has no effect on the education of a Christian. Anything that so closely affects his daily life and that involves him with many other people has a very profound effect on his attitude to his work, his neighbours, and the society in which he lives. Those who have any concern with other aspects of his adult education, cultural, political, theological, must take account of this inescapable and most formative part of his education, which is all the more dominant because the welfare of his family depends on it.

A man must take his own vocational training seriously. He should see it not merely as a means of being equipped for his job. He should also take account of the wider aspects of his training, and of his job, in its effects on himself and on others. He should feel free to criticize his training both as regards its efficiency and its bearing on the common good and on the wider life of the world. He should feel free to ask questions and to make suggestions.

It is, however, in the *doing* of the job rather than in the training for it that a man's real education lies. His job brings him into responsible relations with other people. Here he learns how people depend on each other and how they can best work together. Here he learns— or fails to learn—something about the nature of justice and mercy, of confession and forgiveness. He learns how to take responsibility or how to avoid it. He learns how to make responsible compromises, or to avoid them.

Here we touch on the very crux of whatever we mean by adult education. Education as most of us think of it—the education of the young, at school and college, in apprentice and professional training—is based on the imparting of the experience of older people. It is the experience of their elders that the young are studying most of the time, even when new knowledge is flooding into the textbooks. During the process, their projects, their achievements, their thinking are tested and judged by the experience of their elders. This lies at the heart of the traditional examination system. (It is against this domination by the experience of their elders that much of the present student revolt is aimed.) But the mark of an *adult* is to be free for responsibility. It is the adult who has to do things for the first time. It is the child who is dominated by experience. So long as we are under training we are reacting to the experience of our elders, but when we have finished our formal training we find ourselves doing things on our own, for the first time, without previous experience. And this happens again every time we are promoted to a new job. This improvisation is the distinctive mark of adult life. This is seen in the two most personal actions of adult life—marriage and parenthood. The trial trip is the real thing. There is an infinity of difference between doing things in training under supervision and doing the same thing on one's own, knowing that one has alone to bear the responsibility of mistake. It is in this uncomfortable improvisation of adult life that most of us learn responsibility and find our place in society and know ourselves to be men.

In the local church. But where does the local church come in in all this? The men or women we are talking about—who watch TV and read the papers and do things with their neighbours—these make up the membership of the Church. This is what the word 'layman' implies. It does not mean a man who is right outside the Church and would never think of having anything to do with it, though quite often we seem to use it with this meaning. It means a member, and generally today a non-ordained member, of the Church of Jesus Christ, whatever his record of attendance at a local church may be. So when we are considering how the place where he lives and works is where, for better or for worse, he receives his basic training as an adult Christian, then his local church should have an important part in this. But does it? Many—especially working men—do not feel that it does. They feel that its contribution is negative, preventing them from doing things, preventing them from making experiments, preventing them from asking questions. Their frustration is the sign that they feel that they *ought* to find in a local church more adequate training for life. They look to the local church in vain for training for responsibility in the world. *Particularly they look for training for action in their immediate situation.*

Revolutionary prophets with their blueprints of what the Church ought to do, and ecclesiastical leaders with their dogmatic statements of what they think the ecumenical church already is, are often exasperated by the insistence of ordinary men and women on discussing nothing but the failure or the comfortable little successes of their local church. But these people are often right. If the local church fails the whole Church fails. If the local church is not equipping its members for the life of the world, then there will have to be a revolution in the life of the local church as well as in the total structure of the Church. Whatever happens, *some form of local grouping will emerge for the self-education of Christians in their immediate situation.*

The local church should, therefore, be the basic place for the formation of the adult Christian. It has even in its present form distinct advantages to offer, even though it does not always recognize them or often use them. It is corporate and offers involvement at various levels with other people. It is set in an actual physical neighbourhood. It has something of a common basis of faith from which it can go out in action.

But before we go on to think of the ways by which the local church can share in the education of its members, there are one or two things that we should note.

The local church must not regard itself as self-sufficient. It must never stand in the way of a Christian's sense of being a member of the one universal Church.

We sometimes talk of the local church being the local manifestation of the one universal Church. This is flying a bit too high and can be very misleading. There should always be in the mind of a member of a local church the knowledge that the Church of God to which he belongs is vastly bigger than his local church and also the knowledge that there are in his vicinity a great number of other groups of Christians from whom he must not divide himself. Clergy often forget that though they naturally lead their lives in denominational separation the laity are only segregated from their other Christian neighbours and fellow workers by the tragic denominational requirements of Sunday mornings. The local church has no more right than the nation to a Christian's absolute loyalty. The local church is an institution with a certain purpose, and unless it fulfils that purpose it has no right to exist.

The local church has, therefore, to justify its presence. It is not enough just to be there. It is not the eternal Church. It is only the changing form that the Church has adopted to serve its purpose in a certain place at a certain time. It is there to serve the people of the locality by acting its love and manifesting its faith and by offering to men the wonder of worship, and the main purpose of its corporate life is to educate and sustain its members in their work in the world.

The local church has the right to ask for the service of some of its members in order that it may do its job efficiently. It needs people to run its administration, to assist in its worship, to care for those in need, and to help to educate its members, young and adult. There are few places where these things could not be done much better than they are at present. There are few places where there are not available untapped sources of trained help. But however well the work of the local church is done, this work can and should involve only a few people out of its total membership, and they must not be allowed to make this 'housekeeping' the main end and activity of church life.

The local church, therefore, must not make excessive demands on the time of its members. It must be sure that its activities are significant and useful to its members in their life in the world. It should ask of any of its activities, not 'Why don't people support this properly?' but 'Why do we do this?'

What, then, are the ways in which the local church can be a 'school in the Lord's service' for its members?

First of all, the local church can be the place where people can study the meaning of their life and of their faith today, freely and openly and *with the intention of acting as a result of this study*. No one would say that this is easy. Nor would anyone claim that this kind of study is commonly found in local churches today. Yet it is one of the main justifications of gathering people together in a local congregation. It involves asking questions freely and seeking honest answers. In many churches this is not easy because people think that to ask a question is to confess to doubts of the faith. It's not that there are no questions in their minds but simply that they have not been led to see that their questions are quite proper, and indeed arise out of their faith. Common membership of a local church should give people an open freedom in asking questions and in seeking answers. Where would you expect to find questions asked and new ideas expressed about medicine but among doctors, or about law but among lawyers, or about physics but among physicists? Where should you expect to hear new questions asked and new ideas expressed about the Christian faith but in the Church? But do you? You will only get such free discussion where people feel that they have a right to ask questions, and where they have the experience to test their answers.

For open discussion also demands a willingness to hear opinions from all sides. There is, no doubt, a place for a course of study on such topics as 'the Bible in the light of modern scholarship'. But the moment when a real theological discussion will emerge into life will be when people begin to discuss freely the problems of their jobs and the questions that face their daily world, and when they realize both that no one can give them a slick answer and that the only answers that matter will be expressed in action. It is here that questions about the way we think about God and how we read the Bible and what prayer means will make a full theological impact. The congregation of the local church can be in the unique position of being able to do this. It contains a variety of people. It can have a sense of commitment that saves discussion from being purely academic. It has a basis of common faith that should make it easy to ask questions. The local church often has all these things; but generally it does not know that it has them. It is often up to the laity to demonstrate the potentiality of the local church. They alone can make the discussion relevant.

Secondly, the local church is the place that should be able to educate its members in responsibility.

The responsible person is one who knows that he must do something, and is able to make up his mind what to do. It must be confessed that the Church in the last hundred years has failed in the teaching of responsible action and decision-making. Rather it has given its members the idea that it is better to keep an open mind than to risk making up one's mind, and that the safest thing to do is nothing.

But the Christian faith—and life itself—is a matter of making choices and taking decisions. And the congregation should be the place that trains us to do this. Of course, the local church sees its place in many of the most important decisions of a man's life, as when he confesses his faith or when he gets married. But it has done little to help a man to make decisions in the daily affairs of life—how he spends his time and his money, how he chooses a job, how he educates his children. It may call on him at times to try to take decisions on great world issues—on war and peace, on world hunger, and on world government. But unless a man has got into the way of making responsible decisions in his local daily life he is not likely to be able to take responsible decisions in public life. If he lets his neighbours decide how he spends his time and his money he will let the daily press decide his political opinions. The local church should be the place where Christians are able to discuss together how they should come to their decisions and make their choices. This does not mean that a man necessarily has to submit to the decisions of a group. It does mean that in coming to his own decisions he will have the help of knowing how other people came to theirs.

The local church can also give training for corporate action. There are sometimes actions in local social and political life which the local church should feel called upon to undertake or to initiate. At the moment it is often very hesitant. Perhaps the young people of the local church take some kind of political action, generally in the form of a demonstration or a protest. Or, more often, they do something of a social nature, such as re-decorating old people's homes or visiting hospitals. Their elders in the church regard these activities with patronizing eyes : the protests with sour comments and the social work, perhaps, with rather more approval. They'll say, 'It may be useful training for young people, but in any case they will grow out of it.' They do not seem to realize that the reason why young people often do odd things is that they rarely see their elders do anything at all.

But the most significant actions in which local church people can engage are *those in which they co-operate with other members of the community*. Nothing is more needed for an active lay obedience than that Christians learn to live and work with those of other faiths and other opinions. In the past church members have often been discouraged from working with those of other beliefs. It is still sometimes regarded as questionable that a member of the church should join a political party, because he will have to associate with non-Christians. This is particularly true of the church at the local level. We have, fortunately, got to the stage where the local church now realizes that it must work with those of other Christian denominations. We have a long way to go before we learn to work with all other people without distinction. This is a necessary but difficult task for the local church.

This is all the more urgent because the local church is still often in a unique position to initiate local co-operative activities. The difficulty that people have in working together is by no means confined to the Church. It is evident all through our society, and often the Church is the only body that can gather together all those who are concerned about the life of the community. In many places a local church has been the means of bringing together social and medical workers, teachers, and probation officers, and local councillors, and at the first meeting has found that such people had never met together before.

Thirdly, worship has a major place in the educational work of the local church. We have already discussed the place of worship in the life of a Christian. This we now take for granted, and here we have only to discuss the place of worship in the local training of an adult Christian.

Participation in worship has its obvious place in training and sustaining members of a local church in their faith. But if what is demanded of them is only the passive duty of attendance, and if the content of worship seems but slightly related to their daily lives, worship may actually be a major block in their education for responsible activity in the world. New ways must be found to relate their worship to their daily lives, and to stimulate their imaginations and commitment.

As an example of what might be done, we take the 'Christian Year'. This is generally accepted as one of the best ways by which the central beliefs of the Christian faith are brought regularly to the attention of worshippers. But it has become rather a sacred cow. It tends to prevent the thinking out of the meaning of the faith for men today.

There are many reasons for this.

One is that no one quite knows what it means. As the sequence of teaching concentrates on Christmas and Easter it is often thought of as an attempt to cover the life of Jesus. But this is most confusing to ordinary people. You can't commemorate a man's life in a year. And this is made the more difficult in that we celebrate the birth of Jesus in December and his death three months later and are left with the rest of the year rather blank. We are not often helped to see that the 'Christian year' with which we are dealing is not a potted version of the life of Jesus but is the actual year in which we are living. The Christian Year is this year of grace—1971, 1984, 2000. It is certainly not obvious to people that the Christian Year can be a means by which we tie down our faith and our worship to the contemporary situation today.

Some efforts are, of course, made to bring the modern world into the Christian Year. We have United Nations Day. We have Mother's Day. We have, in each denomination, days which seek to harness the attention and generosity of members to some scheme or concern of the Church. The demand for such days is right; though it is doubtful whether they can be fitted any longer into a scheme which is archaic, devotionally and liturgically.

A complete rethinking of the year's programme of worship and teaching would be a useful exercise for members of a local church. They would have to think what they were doing and why. The worship would become theirs. And if every local church in an area had a different pattern, what would it matter? A minimum uniformity would be preserved by Christmas and Easter and other major festivals and holidays.

One of the results of such fresh planning would be that we might escape from our present practice of concentrating on *preparations* for Christmas in Advent and for Easter in Lent, and could give some time to considering the *consequences* of Christmas and Easter on our lives. An intelligent scheme for a year's worship would have of course to take account of holidays and working habits, and in so doing it would be able to relate what is done in worship to the public and industrial life of the locality, and not merely to the traditional devotional habits of some church people.

And it is quite likely that our concentration on Sunday will have to go. The week as a unit of time is bound to decrease in importance in the life of modern man. It is not a natural unit like the day or the month or the year. Automation is already upsetting it. Sunday as the only day of rest in a six-day working week has long been superseded by Saturday and Sunday, and now the longer weekend is upsetting the old pattern still more. It may be that we shall have to think out new occasions and new seasons for worship, related to our secular timetable and our modern concerns rather than to the agricultural timetable of an age that is past and to the religious needs of an uneducated rural society. Perhaps only as we free people from the tyranny of Sunday—the same activity every Sunday—will they be able to participate in wider social activities, and will the local church at the same time find a renewed life and purpose.[1]

1. There are local churches in California, in Minnesota, and elsewhere, which have abandoned Sunday as the main day for worship, since so many of their congregation are away from

We have considered the question of the Christian Year and the use of Sunday, not only because they are important in themselves but because they illustrate the way in which lay participation in preparations for worship can result in important discussions on belief and on action. This is where the laity make their significant contribution to worship. It is good that lay people should share and be seen to share in the conduct of worship by, for instance, reading the lessons and taking the offering and preaching. But their significant contribution is not in these things but in their participation in the discussion of what worship is about and the content it should have. In this way the experience and thinking of the laity can make its creative contribution to the worship of the local church. And at the same time the worship of the local church can play an important part in the education of the laity.

There are other things to be considered too, such as the use of films and drama, and coffee houses for the young, which are dealt with in detail in the books mentioned in the Bibliography for this chapter. One other educational influence of the local church is often forgotten. We know now more clearly than ever before the good or bad educational influences exercised by the architecture, the symbols, and the ritual of both the social and the religious life of a local church. Does the shape of the building suggest the whole people of God doing something of great importance together, or some specially important Christians (clergy, choir) far away at the east end vitally concerned in some rather obscure mysteries, while the congregation are seated way back in the nave as passive spectators of the service? (For instance, Coventry Cathedral was in fact designed as one

---

home on that day. Instead, they attempt to make a mid-week evening the accepted time for all church members to come together for worship and education.

of the last *old-fashioned* cathedrals in the country, and in consequence the present staff, who are desperately concerned to overcome the difficulties of the long narrow structure, and to involve all the congregation in active worship, often prefer not to use the high altar.) What do the stained-glass windows, the Old Testament and New Testament symbolism, the design and printing and language of prayerbooks and hymnbooks teach people? How are the congregation seated, how welcome are outsiders made? What are the notice-boards and the church porch like? Many men and women pass by churches day after day, though they go into them seldom. What impression of unity or of division, of welcome or of exclusiveness, of efficiency or of sloppiness do they get?

These are some of the ways in which the local church can play a significant part in the adult education of its members and of people in the local community. These should never take up much of their time. The immediate locality to which a man belongs is so determinative of his life that the things he does there must be significant; but they are not all-engrossing. There are other things that the local church cannot do. He must do these outside. He must be given time to do them outside.

9. The Local Church Cannot Do Everything

The local church, then, can undertake a good deal of laity education, and indeed it is likely to survive as an indispensable structure for many Christians for a good time to come. Some of the radical reformers have been very premature (and tactless) in pronouncing that 'the parish is finished'. But the local congregation no longer has a monopoly of laity education, and this it must admit.

In the days of the Middle Ages, when the structure of parishes throughout Europe was one of the finest networks of human organization that has ever been achieved, the parish was everything to most men. You lived and slept there, you worked, played, and had your local politics there. The village, or the mediaeval city parish, which was also very small and compact, represented almost all your interests. (There are still men and women living in parts of Britain and Europe who have never moved outside their parish.) In these circumstances, the local church provided an education, formal or informal, which covered all your interests and the whole of your life. Only the lord of the manor, and one or two other important people, and perhaps a few young men who went away as soldiers, knew the wider world outside. (And they had their chaplains, their non-parochial ministers to serve them.) The village contained not only your domestic and neighbourhood responsibilities, but your work, your leisure and your politics, too. And so the local church could in one way or another educate you in almost all the obligations and opportunities of your life.

But today most of us do not live in villages; and if we do we move outside them almost every week; and the world of Saigon and Glasgow and Chicago comes to us every evening in the TV news. This means that some of us live in many 'parishes', many areas of life and responsibility. A man may have his home in a Connecticut suburb, work in New York City (and fly to Chicago or London during the week), spend his weekends with relatives in New Jersey or at a summer home in Maine, find his vacations in Florida (and plan to retire there), devote his spare time to a city bar association, and get involved in national Republican party politics. A working woman in South London may spend her weekends with a married sister in Kent, holiday each year in Cornwall, and be keenly interested in a spastics society with a central London headquarters. She is also thinking of joining her union, if she can find the time to go to meetings. All these connections, which are commonplace for more and more people in modern society, take us away from our residential parish both physically and psychologically. And for these interests there must be appropriate styles of Christian education.

It is very likely that a good local parish may offer suitable education for three of the main areas of lay education which we listed in Chapter 8. It can, especially if it makes ecumenical links with other local churches, give much help in understanding :

(1) church duties,

(2) family responsibilities,

and

(3) the local neighbourhood.

(This may easily involve the local parish in some sharp controversy on local issues such as housing, race discrimination, the quality of education in local schools, and so on. We certainly do not suggest that the local church can avoid local political and controversial issues.)

It is, however, likely that the local church cannot cope adequately with all the problems of :

(4) responsibilities in work, business, commerce, and economic organization,

(5) leisure,

and

(6) the tremendous political and public responsibilities of men today. These are not just the obligations of a village, or suburb, or township, or small town. They inevitably reach to the metropolis, to the county and state and nation, and further still.

Many local parsons have to learn to accept these limitations on their parish's role in Christian education. It has a place, but no longer a monopoly, in such matters.

There is a strong analogy here with the development of secular education in the last hundred years. The days of the self-contained rural parish were also the days of the small local one-room school and the little red schoolhouse of American Mid-Western mythology. Then, all the children were taught together, and the syllabus was relatively simple. Even then some promising scholars went on to college; just as from the parish an occasional bright boy moved on to theological seminary. Today, secular education has exploded into a rich variety of different educational institutions for people of different abilities and interests. We do not dream of trying to keep all education local, nor complain when boys and girls move on to specialized education, even far from home. In the same way, while the local church can do a little for almost everybody, and much more for some parishioners (locally centred housewives, senior citizens, and so on), it must allow many of its members to move on to more specialized styles of Christian education.

Indeed, many men in the churches are profoundly bored by the rather naïve and very general talks about the laity which they suffer during parish programmes. They have heard it all before. They want to move on to much more detailed and technical discussions on what it means to be a real-estate agent in Los Angeles or Wolverhampton, what kinds of responsible compromises a drug salesman has to accept, what a doctor does about terminal illnesses. They want to meet their peers, and a few people more experienced in their particular responsibilities. They want to talk about these things competently and often confidentially (and certainly not with a general mixed group of rather uninformed parishioners). They see no earthly reason why such discussions should be denominationally exclusive. The problems of a Presbyterian teacher in a city university are not very different from those of a Methodist. A Roman Catholic technologist has the same questions about the awesome power he is dealing with as a Lutheran. They need, *not instead of but as well as their residential parish*, other opportunities of ecumenical education and support.

Incidentally, though these needs are particularly felt by professional and political people, there is also a need for specialized styles of Christian education for at least some working-class men—blue-collar workers. Such men —and working women too—often feel ill at ease at the nice, rather prissy, 'respectable' style of parish groups. They do not always join naturally with others in the Sunday congregation, and their natural gossip (and therefore 'dialogue') groupings may be fitted more to the café where they have a meal, or the pub or club where they have a drink. We are not for one moment suggesting that working men should be haunted by self-conscious do-good ministers whenever they repair to their favourite local for relaxation; but much experience in industrial centres such as Manchester or Detroit has shown that the traditional parish breaks down in attempting to offer Christian education and fellowship not only to business executives jetting round the world, but also to working men, shop stewards, steel workers, and the like.

It seems to us that many parish clergy ought now to consider themselves, not as educational monopolists, but as educational counsellors. For instance, we may expect that Mr Smith, in charge of a reasonably flourishing suburban parish in Surrey, keeps proper parish records. He will know the names and addresses of his parishioners, the amount they 'pledge' to keep the parish going, their families, and something of their personal circumstances. We hope, too (but not so certainly), that he has a note of their jobs, and of their major public and political interests. We must hope, also, that he has details of *all the opportunities for adult Christian education* that each has had in the past.

A few will stand out as 'conference haunters', rather sad types who are hooked on Christian conferences as others may take an annual health cure. A fair number will have had some systematic Christian education through special parish events, such as Lenten courses. A large number will have had no major experience of learning an adult understanding of the faith since boyhood days, maybe five, maybe thirty-five years ago. They are in great danger of fossilization in a world which calls for all men to be constantly learning and constantly curious.

Once a parson and his church wardens (or deacons, or what have you) have assembled this kind of data, so that they may know the interests, the strengths, and the weaknesses of their laity, then they should quite calmly work out what the local church can and cannot do to remedy the gaps that will surely be apparent. And they should know where to find other kinds of Christian education to fill the gaps that their local church cannot itself satisfy. Mrs X has a real need for family counselling, and this St Marmaduke's can supply itself. Mr Y is a journalist on the evening paper, determined to make a career of this but worried about the rubbish his paper prints every night in order to stay alive. (Not many journalists will ever work for the *Guardian* or the *New York Times*.) His dilemmas are not easily explained to the general mixed laity in the congregation : he desperately needs to find a supportive and critical group of Christian journalists, somewhere within a one-hundred-mile radius, where he can hammer out his Christian commitment and maybe swear a little, drink a little, and pray a little. His parish simply cannot provide this for him (or similar opportunities for Mrs G who is a psychiatrist, for Mr K who wonders whether he can stand working any longer at the town hall, and for Miss S who wants desperately to experiment in new styles of religious drama).

Every parish, then, ought to allow and indeed to encourage many of its laity to seek other opportunities for specialized education, without labelling them as 'disloyal' because they do not always come to parish programmes. Indeed, it ought to be proud that its members sometimes move on to 'advanced' programmes, instead of trying to keep them in local and rather elementary groups. It would be very good if sometimes a parish offered scholarship money or travel grants for younger church members, to make them more able to engage in such advanced education—just as in the past some parishes used to help with college expenses for promising young men and women (and not only for seminary training). And the parish leaders ought sometimes to ask a man to give them a brief report on his national conference or his vocational group, so that they can see how such a programme might help another parishioner later.

All this means that the whole Church of God is now quite properly multiple in structure, and that many people (both laity and clergy) will have membership of more than one form of Christian fellowship and nurture. It is quite likely that a man will have not only :

(1) a residential congregation to belong to,
and perhaps

(2) a second residential congregation to join when he is at his country cottage or away for the weekend. (This phenomenon is common in some areas of the United States and Canada, and is coming on to the horizon in many of the more affluent areas of Britain and Europe.) He may also have :

(3) a vocational group for doctors, lawyers, or teachers to attend,
and perhaps

(4) a public interest group—on poverty, or overseas aid, or slum housing—to meet with.

It is, of course, unlikely that Christian groups 3 and 4 will meet weekly; for a monthly obligation—or even a weekend two or three times a year—often fits their diaries better. Any membership of a 'vacation' church (2) is also likely to be spasmodic. But it is now hopelessly unrealistic to imagine that a layman can exist and can be happy with only his 'dormitory' church (1) to support and educate him.

It may also be emphasized that such Christian groups as 3 and 4 will very soon attract many 'fringe' Christians who have almost entirely opted out of the residential congregations (1 and 2). There is at the moment a great deal of radical thinking about the future structure of the whole Church of God for its life in the world tomorrow (in ecumenical jargon 'the missionary structure of the congregation', to quote the title of a study recently sponsored by the World Council of Churches). Laity education is obviously a major element in any such new structure, and we would here only emphasize that any monopolistic solution is likely to be unsatisfactory. Some 'churchless' Christians today are just Christian individualists; but many more are simply unable to be satisfied with only what they find in residential congregations (1 and 2). They may be much more ready to join in informal 'churches' or groups like 3 and 4, and it would be wiser for church leaders to recognize this in a relaxed and even grateful way than to abuse them for not being keener members of the choir or the women's sewing circle.

It is, incidentally, a great pity that in some churches, especially Roman Catholic ones, the whole matter of informal church groups is sometimes confused and romanticized by calling them 'underground' churches. Certainly there are problems of Catholic church law and authority to be argued about; and the same kinds of questions come up in both tedious and tragic ways when almost any ecumenical group wishes to celebrate Communion together as a mark of their fellowship and concern. But it is very difficult to maintain today that there is anything wrong or 'illegal' in Christian people—especially the laity—engaging in informal education, discussion, reflection, and even prayer together. There should be no need for them to be secretive or 'underground' about this.

10. Do You Need a Residential Centre?

When after 1945 the movement towards new styles of laity education got under way in Europe, it was often assumed that these would take place in some kind of special building. Generally a German 'academy'[1] or Dutch lay centre was started in some semi-rural setting, a long way (sometimes a very long way) from the bustle and train services of a great city. At first large old country houses were much in vogue, and indeed in Germany this was almost the only kind of unbombed accommodation which could be obtained. Later, as for instance at Loccum and Arnoldshain, fine new special purpose buildings were erected.

In recent years there has been much argument about all this, and about the need for yet more church expenditure on real estate. In our opinion there is no simple general 'Yes' or 'No' to the question: 'Do you need a special building for lay education?' In each local situation and for each specific proposal, there is need for a very careful analysis of the pros and cons. We would only suggest here some of the major questions to be faced, and the major arguments often advanced on either side.

For a special building. A major part of the case for a special Christian building for Christian education is

1. European lay centres are often called 'academies' after the German title *Evangelische Akademie*. These are not 'evangelical boarding schools' of any description, but Protestant (*Evangelische*) discussion and education centres. (The German word *Akademie* relates to the Greek and Socratic insistence on having a place for argument and dialogue.)

based on the psychological need for a special 'atmosphere' of community and fellowship together. Presumably nobody nowadays will insist that Christians can *only* think and reflect and pray properly in a building which has been specially consecrated and dedicated by a priest; but this does not mean that a building and physical plant cannot 'grow' a certain style of community life and an atmosphere of spiritual ease. Much human experience indicates that there are styles of accommodation, of decoration, and of domestic organization that provide a certain ambience (whether this be for a restaurant or a hospital) that helps human beings to adapt to the business in hand. In a special building, too, it is much easier to make provision for worship and for quiet; and without subscribing to superstitious beliefs about the special 'holiness' of a chapel it is clear to many experimenters that effective meditation may be more easily achieved in a room designed for prayer and worship than in a hotel room or a lecture theatre. By all accounts, there is something about a centre for reflection like St Julian's in Sussex, England or the Bergamo centre for Christian renewal in Dayton, Ohio which attracts not only what may be called 'religiously minded' people but also many quite secularly oriented laymen.

A special centre also provides a physical base for staff and volunteer helpers, who may otherwise have a very restless time, physically, moving from one place to another without any working base. It helps to grow a reliable and faithful group of friends and supporters (and if some of this involvement is rather romantic and unintellectual, it may still be genuine and helpful). A country centre can provide much refreshment for people normally cramped by city squalor and suburban trivialities, and the psychology of getting away from it all for a time can help to encourage a good fresh look at the urban responsibilities to which we must return. It can provide this, and opportunity for relaxation as well, below the high costs of family holidays in commercially run centres.

The Case Against. Many of those who are determined not to get involved in the problems of running physical plant attack this very matter of a 'Christian atmosphere' in such places. They do not find it attractive at all. This is especially true when rather 'worldly' young clergy or laity, immersed in the *mores* as well as the problems of modern city life, trudge out to Christian Comfort Farm in deepest Gloucestershire or arrive late (for it is far from an airport) at Lake Methuselah, Wyoming. They are expected to sing hymns before supper, they are not encouraged to smoke, and the nearest alcohol is far too far away (and, officially, forbidden). In such circumstances, they do not feel at ease at all; indeed they often lose their tempers. Romans and Anglicans are often allowed rather more 'worldly' pleasures, but may be called to suffer instead a great emphasis on traditional liturgical worship, in which they may feel they are asked to admit to improbable sins in cold chapels at unreasonable hours several times a day.

It is, frankly, very difficult to design a Christian centre in which old and young, traditional and radical theologians, puritans and permissive types can all fit in. Some would say that this simply presents more opportunities for genuine Christian hospitality in a centre, and some chances for reconciliation between the different styles of life which now exist within the one great Christian Church. Others would insist that the problem presents such difficulties that the solution is impossible, and that they, at least, would wish to avoid the heavy liabilities of running a centre altogether.

Another and important argument against special Christian centres is the economic one. It really is very expensive to run a residential educational centre, with anything like the necessary standards of comfort, in the middle of nowhere. This is particularly true when one works out (as one should) the true 'bed usage' and the true economic costs per bed-night over the year. By the nature of things, lay education conferences tend to be concentrated at weekends, and during certain periods of the year. It is likely that many centres will have beds empty during the week, especially in November and February. Far too many leaders of lay centres are having to run around finding anybody, yes anybody, who will use their buildings during the 'off periods'. They find themselves in the conference business, trying to get salesmen to plan toothpaste sales campaigns on their premises (and playing down the puritan atmosphere a little), urging clergy and church bureaucrats and retired people to come and use the plant during the week (and sometimes thereby twisting and distorting the whole flavour of the total programme, so that lay people begin to avoid 'that churchy place in Blankshire with religious widows always hanging about'). The 'anti-centre' party will certainly insist on a comparison between the real costs of hiring secular accommodation (even at seemingly high charges) *just for the nights it is needed*, and the total year-round expenses of keeping a residential centre open, whether it is used or not.

They will claim that a major advantage of renting space in a hotel or a motel is that everybody can choose —and pay for—his own standard of comfort and behaviour. If he wants to telephone long-distance, buy a few drinks, and have a private bathroom, then he can; and the conference leaders are not necessarily embarrassed or bankrupt by this. And the businessman, or politician, or industrialist, is relieved to know that he does not have to return to Boy Scout days and sleep in a long multi-bed dormitory.

We would very much like to see some attempts to make experimental arrangements with commercial motels or hotels. Except in holiday areas and in the tourist season, many perfectly respectable and comfortable hotels have low occupancy rates on Friday and Saturday nights; for businessmen do everything they can to get home for the weekend. Their conference rooms, too, are less in demand (except perhaps for wedding receptions). It should be possible for Christian educationalists to come to an arrangement to have an office at one end of the hotel, and to have the use of bedrooms and conference rooms, at very attractive rates, for the weekends. A little skill in temporary furnishings for the conference rooms can make them very suitable for both discussions and informal worship, so long as they are quiet and undisturbed and have suitable lighting. In the United States and Canada, since new motels are always being erected and opened, it might be possible to incorporate some special points in their design from the start, especially if the proprietor or manager has some genuine interest in the project.

In Britain, the slow progress in hotel and motel construction makes such an idea less likely to be practicable, in the immediate future. But when, inevitably, the motel idea spreads over the British Isles, there may be room for such experimentation. In any case, the 'anti-centre' people will urge, in Britain as across the Atlantic, a ruthless look at economic costs. No false affection for St Ermentrude's retreat centre must avoid consideration of how much it costs to keep it open (and what that money could do elsewhere). No tactful appreciation of Mrs Mugg's generosity in leaving her venerable castle to the Church in her will must stop a calm assessment of how much it will cost to heat, furnish, deworm, and staff Mugg's Hall as a Christian residential centre.

As we have seen, the advantages of having some special premises for lay education are largely psychological. If, therefore, it is decided that it is worth while having the expense and responsibilities of special church property for such purposes, then the style of its equipment and operation is extremely important. A church centre with a poor, uncomfortable, inhibiting style of work is a dreadful handicap to lay education.

To some extent the buildings and equipment required will depend on the use to which they will be put. Very few lay education projects are so well financed that their leaders can be perfectionists about this, even in Germany or in the United States. It is, indeed, very bad steward-ship of money and resources to plan the construction or adaptation of buildings with so narrow a use in mind that they stay empty a great deal of the time. There are four main possibilities for lay centres, and the style both of their furnishings and their operation will vary a cer-tain amount according to the type of work undertaken.

1. There are now many lay centres mainly devoted to formal or informal education of the laity, with a good deal of emphasis on lectures, group discussions, and so on. There are over fifty of these in Europe (joined to-gether in the Association of Lay Centres in Europe); and many more in other countries. The World Council of Churches publication *Centres of Renewal* gives some de-tails of these (see the Bibliography for this chapter).

2. Other centres concentrate more on worship, prayer, and the retreat type of programme. These are centres which aim more at opportunities for reflection and meditation—either corporate or individual—than at ex-periences in Christian controversy (though they do not always wish or find it possible to avoid these!). Ex-amples of such work are to be found at the Swedish centre at Rättvik, the Benifold centre in southern Eng-land, and such American centres as Yokefellow House, Richmond, Indiana and Kirkridge, Pennsylvania.

3. A third type of centre wishes above all to give its guests some chance of physical rest and relaxation—and it is difficult to overestimate the value of these services to many laymen. There are many testimonies to the value of St Julians, in Sussex, England; and many of the holiday-

camp or chalet centres in the United States offer a great opportunity for individual and family relaxation, with a certain minimum of spiritual refreshment—short evening services, a chaplain available for personal counselling, and maybe one or two visiting speakers during the week. In the USA, there can be certain tensions between the expectations of the guests (who perhaps want to be left alone) and the organizers, who feel vaguely that they must offer 'uplift' at regular intervals : the great blessing of a place like St Julians is that you really can find peace and quiet without being disturbed or organized.

4. A fourth type of centre offers not physical rest but physical exhaustion as a means of lay renewal. These are the centres where you hump stones about for the good of your soul, and maybe suffer extremes of temperature and simple cooking to appease your guilt feelings about the affluent society. Such asceticism, provided it does not extend to pneumonia and indigestion, undoubtedly helps some people to new freshness and vigour. But such a centre is not for everyone, no more than hill walking, skiing, or mountaineering. Some people found the early days on Iona excessively uncomfortable : others felt that the working and conference weeks in the pioneer years of the Iona Community were extraordinarily valuable. Other such programmes are those of St David's Community in West Wales, and the outdoor activities weeks of the Scargill Community in Wharfedale, Yorkshire.

We would suggest that whatever the style of programme to be offered at a residential centre, things will normally go much better if certain basic human needs are met. One of these, especially in Britain, is plenty of warmth when the weather is bad. It is also extremely doubtful whether bad cooking helps to forward the cause of good dialogue. Even if the centre must be run on very economical lines, the simple life does not have to mean poorly cooked and served meals. We would also venture to suggest that some centres, at least, should be more free to experiment in offering a little alcoholic refreshment as part of their hospitality. This of course is impossible in the centres which follow rigorously the teetotal tradition of some British and American denominations; *and it is only good manners for others who visit them to recognize this.* On the other hand, Anglican, Lutheran, and Roman Catholic churches have never tried to enforce such a blanket prohibition of drinking; and there is no doubt that a reasonable amount of such refreshment during a conference, as at a German academy or, say, William Temple College, has done a good deal to put lay people at their ease. (It is sometimes maintained that the 'happy hour' at an Episcopalian conference in the United States—i.e. the period of pre-dinner drinks— does much more to get the group adjusted to each other than any group dynamics process.) It is sometimes the case that to prohibit drinking—and even smoking—at a Christian education or youth centre does emphasize the psychological tensions between such attitudes and the normal background of many 'fringe laymen' who may hopefully attend conferences and courses there. Some will maintain, of course, that this is a proper price to pay for maintaining proper traditions of church behaviour. It is certainly a fairly high one.

Most important of all, in all centres and in all situations, is to have a really friendly welcome from the staff. The difference between first-class and bottom-class Christian hospitality is vast, and it is made up of countless small things : the first greetings when you arrive in the entrance hall, often rather tired after an extraordinary journey (should there not be a competition for the most-difficult-to-get-to centre in the Christian Church?); the tone and style of the inevitable notices—and whether some of them can be found in more than one language— not all the visitors to European centres speak English or German; the way in which people answer your telephone enquiries—or leave the 'phone ringing. Of course most of these are the points which make a good hotel stand out among the mediocre ranks of its competitors; and extra hymn singing will not save a Christian residential centre from damnation if it does not learn the art of hospitality, even for paying guests. It is an old story that many veteran pilgrims when they get to heaven always ask for a good Swiss hotel. A sacramental view of the holiness of common things ought to extend to hospitality.

Beyond these basic essentials, additional comforts and facilities will depend very much on your expected uses for the property. If you are really going in for 'roughing it', then little more may be needed beyond log huts, good fires, a cheerful and unflappable warden, and plenty to eat. It is worth mentioning that such youth-hostel-style accommodation can often be sited in a corner of the estate of a major centre. It then provides for younger visitors and youth groups somewhere where they can pursue their own quiet or noisy concerns away from the main house. The youth houses at Boldern, Switzerland, and the youth huts on Iona are valuable examples of this.

For all other centres, it is increasingly necessary to move away from the youth hostel, YMCA, creaky-bunk-beds-in-large-cold-rooms style of operation. One of the difficulties in taking over Woodworm Castle or Plutocrat Hall is that they seldom have enough small rooms. Yet very few adults now, outside a war emergency, have experience of sleeping a dozen to a room together. Of course everyone can survive an uncomfortable night; but it is no gain to your conference to have some people short of sleep and temper until they can get back home. Sometimes such spartan accommodation may be necessary, but it is a pity to plan a centre to be uncomfortable from the start, even if you are training Christian revolutionaries.

Whether or not you have a separate chapel or quiet room will depend on your past traditions and your present theology. (More, we hope, on the latter than on the former.) We would simply urge that there be ample provision, in the house, somehow or other, for quiet and for reflection. In Britain, at any rate, it is a sad mistake to assume that the weather will always allow communion with God in the open air. If guests are to think things over in their bedrooms, then they must probably be single rooms, well soundproofed and with some kind of desk and a comfortable chair. A good many people doodle, scribble, and so on when they are reflecting: they certainly don't spend all the time on their knees. If there is to be a chapel, then let it be quiet, warm, and reasonably comfortable for reading. If there is no formal chapel, then it may be good to have a quiet room, with a silence rule very strictly maintained.

If many centres have a chapel, not enough have what we may call a 'secular contact room'. A time for retreat is not a chance for a Christian to withdraw from the world to look at his own soul. It is a chance for him to look at the world more calmly and reflectively than usual. A centre needs therefore to have a good choice of non-religious books available—books on town planning, race relations, Africa, drama, poetry (and not only slim volumes written by orthodox Christians). It needs to have good hi-fi equipment, and this must be watched with real scrupulosity so that its quality is not ruined by amateur operators. It needs a good TV set, and a room where this can be enjoyed without disturbing other people. For if some laymen are surfeited with television, and need a breather from regular viewing, a good many of the more 'concerned', over-busy, and church-oriented laity need to watch the box a little more often, so that they can understand the fantastic potentials of this kind of mass medium. And of course we do not mean that they should just watch the religious programmes. It is extraordinarily important that the centre should spend money on a good selection of periodicals (more than denominational journals and *Time*, *Life*, and *Punch*). It is most valuable if there is somewhere an enormous notice-board with news of a wide range of educational and cultural events in the area. It is a fascinating experience to enter a centre like the Roman Catholic Grailville House in Loveland, Ohio, and find there a kaleidoscope of different posters and announcements.

Many of the housekeeping details of lay centres are of less general interest; and further specialized advice about running a lay centre is best got from experts, and by cribbing intelligently from the experiences of both religious and secular conference centres. We would only remark here that there are such wide differences in standards from centre to centre that there ought to be much more cross-fertilization between them. A great deal depends on the cultural background of the staff, on the contribution which women staff and advisers are or are not allowed to make to the way things are run, and on the basic theology behind the operation of the house. If the leaders have a true understanding of the sacramental importance of good design—even for Woolworth's coffee pots—then all will be well.

Finally there are two particular points which seem often to be overlooked in planning a residential centre. One is of the first importance and concerns the staff. Much experience, in the European lay centres in particular, has shown that the intellectual, spiritual, and psychological strains of running a lay academy are severe and profound, especially when finances do not permit really adequate staffing. It is a heavy business to greet and to entertain a new group of laity, weekend after weekend. It is a very difficult intellectual exercise to switch from subject to subject, from Urban Studies to Central Africa to Sex and the Teenager, without lapsing into shallow platitudes—even 'action now' platitudes. It is a tricky business to deal with the slightly neurotic 'conference hounds', who cling to a centre for emotional reasons or loneliness or personal weakness. (They need, of course, counselling and strengthening, but they may easily distort a conference or the whole programme of a house if they come in considerable numbers and haunt the place.) Many lay-centre leaders have personal and financial worries, and career problems. They have become 'fools for Christ' in risking clerical or lay careers in such out-of-the-mainstream jobs. The romanticism of pioneering fades in the damp English countryside in a dismal February, or in the sticky summer heat of a jolly holiday conference in Ohio, or in the tired committee sessions where once again there is no money for essential experiments. Leaders of lay centres have to achieve a very tough self-discipline if they are to survive, and to stay cheerful; and their friends and board chairmen and relations must help them with this. One essential is to get away from the place regularly, even if bankruptcy is near. Another is to have some private quarters, well separated from the conference rooms, where staff can do what they want, and be with their families, and see private friends, and be entirely off duty. There is of course a slight danger that some leaders may use such private quarters as a pretext for retiring too often from the encounters of the conference. It is much more likely that they will not go apart anything like enough to remain fresh and poised for the next discussions and arguments. At least they must have the physical accommodation which makes withdrawal possible. There is a vast spectrum of experience, not only from the lay centres but also from overseas mission compounds and all kinds of secular residential life, to indicate the long-term dangers of immersing oneself wholly, twenty-five hours a day, eight days a week, fifty-five weeks in a year, in any kind of education.

Another point about having a special building for lay

education relates to its location. We have already indicated some of the great advantages of a quiet centre in the country. Very few church leaders seem to have considered the advantages of having centres in the middle of the great cities. There is one famous German academy —at Hamburg—which has for years operated a very successful programme in the middle of the town—using a private hotel next door for bedrooms when they are required (and now using a second house in the countryside as well as the down-town property). The Iona Community has run for many years Community House, Glasgow, as a town centre; and its successes and failures in this work are worth very careful study. But it seems strange to us that—with all the vast amount of down-town church property in Britain, Europe, and North America (much of it scandalously under-used)—so few people have worked out what might be done in new styles of lay education in such places. (For their enterprise in a down-town location, if not for the highly controversial nature of their lay training, the Ecumenical Institute in Chicago surely deserve high marks.) A few churches in most cities like New York and London have spasmodic courses and discussion forums. The new cathedral at Coventry has developed a very fine programme of lay education in the various rooms under and around the great church (originally intended, most of them, just as 'chair stores' and the like). The J. F. Kennedy Hostel for youth conferences and the cathedral restaurant offer most useful facilities to supplement such lay activities. There are of course other city churches which do a bit of lay education—for example Manchester Cathedral has some important university extra-mural classes, the great Catholic cathedrals in Europe have some groups of concerned lay people tucked away somewhere in the corners, and Trinity Church in New York uses a little of its great wealth in supporting some kinds of lay education, including the important Wall Street Ministry to the financial community. The Glide Foundation, in San Francisco, is outstanding in the extent to which it uses the resources of a down-town church for new and experimental social education.

But often so little is done where there are buildings that are adaptable, and even a number of paid staff who fill up their time with services and traditional personal work. One or two Catholic and Anglo-Catholic monasteries and retreat centres working in city locations have some experience in training and strengthening laity who are busy with the world's problems (and even enjoy such proper busyness). But we urgently need more experimentation in urban lay centres. As we shall see in the next chapter, some good urban education can be done without much in the way of buildings, but a modest discussion centre (perhaps without residential accommodation) would be a valuable asset in a city such as Leeds or Manchester or Cincinnati. It has been a great pleasure to learn of the new plans for the famous Carrs Lane Congregational Church in Birmingham. The old building has been pulled down; and on the same central site there is being built a smaller building more suitable for worship, and a considerable suite of ancillary rooms and lounges which have been specially designed for adult education work.

Here again, style is exceedingly important. Many down-town church premises are grubby, shabby, and uncomfortable. They need not be. There is a strange mythology among some city church workers that to keep premises unpainted, dusty, and even insanitary is somehow to identify with the poor of the 1930s or to show that you are concentrating on More Important Things. The result is that to many city workers in Britain the Church is firmly associated with the ugliness, smells, and decay of British Rail at its seediest. If Christians are to ask the world to come and join them in dialogue and education, the least they can do is to offer a clean room, a comfortable chair, and a really good cup of tea or coffee—with a spoon each and a clean, unchipped cup. Of course all city premises get dirty, and must be cleaned and painted. But if Marks and Spencer's can make their visitors welcome, so can the Church. If this means hard and regular do-it-yourself sessions, that is what dedication is about.

11. What You Can Do Without a Centre

The 'academies' and other residential centres in Europe have done fine work in the last twenty years; but their example is not always the best one to follow for the future. Very much can be done in new kinds of laity education without having a residential centre at all—either in the countryside or in the city. Too many projects in laity education in Britain and in the United States—and in Africa and Asia—have hung fire because of endless questions about buildings and the expense of buildings. Sometimes there has been an interesting experiment which has never started serious work because people lost their nerve when they added up the financial estimates for bedrooms, kitchens, and staff. Sometimes experiments in Africa or the Far East have attracted large grants for buildings, but these may be badly out of scale with the likely yearly income from local church or secular sources—and then there are problems of maintenance and continual dependence on foreign aid. Certainly any new project in laity education needs to worry about leadership, recruitment, and its style of work long before—and not after—it decides on expensive buildings of its own.

This is particularly true for the general mass of adult and youth laity. We shall never have elaborate lay colleges for all of these, and if we did have, the style of work in them and the fees which would have to be charged would put off many ordinary people, especially overseas. In the educational explosion that the churches now face, we shall have to improvise, to multiply educational opportunities at a dangerously fast rate, even if we can never find ideally suitable teachers and group leaders and buildings, and even if the educational processes involved turn out to be less than perfect.

This means that for every city, and for most suburbs, there must be area experiments in Christian education, to supplement what the parishes can do. There have been far too few bold experiments in what can actually be achieved with limited resources. There have been pioneering attempts, for instance in Birmingham, in Bristol, in south London, and in Port Glasgow. Some of the industrial missions, at Sheffield (before the tragic collapse of the original team), at Teesside, and in Scotland have gained much experience in moving beyond personal counselling and pastoral work to informal styles of discussion and education. The Young Christian Workers (Roman Catholic in origin), the East Manchester Group ministry, and one or two of the 'new town' ecumenical ministries have had good but limited success with small groups of working men and youths—sometimes meeting in pubs and clubs rather than in church vestries. In the United States some of the industrial missions and ministries report similar progress—in Detroit with blue-collar workers, in Cincinnati and Boston mainly with more educated workers and managers. From time to time a special ecumenical programme, such as the 'People Next Door' campaign organized by the British Council of Churches in 1966–67, or some of the special studies on race or poverty now current in the United States, attract ecumenical groups of Christians in a city or suburban area, as for example the *Malachi* groups in Dayton, Ohio, or the work of Lake Avenue Baptist Church in Rochester, New York. But for every one town that offers a reasonable choice in such laity education, there are hundreds where little or nothing is available. And, at least in Britain, denominational headquarters find it extremely difficult to stimulate local ingenuity and initiative in such matters, even when they are persuaded that this is desirable. Where such groups of laity do exist (often made up of young graduates), their numbers are tiny and their efficiency seems in question.

Such a situation is now inexcusable. It is worth while saying plainly and emphatically that there is a great deal of useful Christian education for both adults and young people which can be organized economically and efficiently in almost any urban situation. Styles of organization and of recruitment, techniques of informal education, specialist advice : all these are available. What is needed very badly is a group of leaders, both clergy and lay, who have the nerve to start and the guts to slog on for a definite experimental period—maybe as long as five years.

Such leadership is undoubtedly much easier to find in the United States or Canada than in Britain, where the small number of competent laity under forty is often overburdened with both church and secular obligations, and where the brighter clergy are similarly over-busy. This is first and foremost a matter of priorities. We suggest that there is an urgent need for both young ministers and young laity—who do see a little what the Church should be about in the future and what Christians may do in the world—to re-examine their time-tables and their engagements, and to see where they can squeeze some time to act as leaders in laity education. Unless we start—fast—to grow a new kind of lay Christian for the future, we shall have to give up all hope of church renewal.

Three or four such leaders—clerical and lay—can make a local team for laity education if they will sacrifice some of their other interests. When they plan some ecumenical education in their area, they will do well to specialize a bit, certainly at first; for they have to aim to go deeper than ordinary parish groups, and it is not easy to gain even moderate competence in secular problems of politics or poverty or housing. Of course the leaders do not have to provide all the input and teaching for their courses. In very many cases, university extra-mural departments can help (as in Manchester and Birmingham), and local teachers and professional people will join in the experiment. Far more civil servants, and doctors and politically involved people will help in these ways than are normally asked.

Although it would be difficult to tackle too many giant topics at once, it may well be important to offer one or two different subjects for experiment rather than concentrate exclusively on one special theme, which may be a little narrow and perhaps a bit too radical for many lay people in the area. Some of the very keen 'new theology' or 'social action' people rightly insist that their concerns are an important part of lay education for the future; but a lay education experiment which *only* deals with these may result in a very narrow basis of support, and frighten away some of the less 'advanced' laity, who may in time move to more revolutionary topics. Some of the radicals in the Church have so little patience in helping the self-education of their more conservative brethren!

An attractive and not too threatening provisional programme should have in it something to attract the 'fringe laity' who are eager for social action, something for young people who are already beyond the scope of parish education programmes, and something to help along ordinary decent lay people, who are confused and sometimes frightened by the decay of traditional religion, and who are not used to professional study-group techniques. It is equally important to work out a careful and intelligent strategy of recruitment. This is where many laity education experiments founder, for they either produce a frighteningly 'religious' group of traditional laity (who come to anything, especially if the TV is dull that night) or the usual rather tired handful of familiar radicals, who need very badly to widen the impact of their discussions and controversies. The usual methods of circularizing ministers and clergy with a vague invitation to 'send someone' or of 'phoning the people you know and asking them to rally to yet one more new cause, are clearly ineffective.

Here the recruitment procedures of the German lay academies are so worth our attention, and these can apply to all kinds of laity education, and not just to recruitment for residential courses. For instance, if there is the possibility of holding a conference of medical doctors to discuss the problems of terminal illnesses, the staff members of an academy do not just design a conference and then ask local ministers to ask doctors to come along. The first thing they do is to meet two or three friendly and competent doctors over a meal. They will suggest that such a conference might be worth while; and the doctors will generally agree, in principle. (For after all, one could hardly be against the idea.) Then the staff members will ask certain sharp and definite questions:

1. Will one of you take the chair for the conference?

2. Will you find a competent doctor to give the first speech—outlining the problems as a doctor, not as a minister, sees them?

3. Will you do the major work of recruiting for the conference, finding doctors who are seriously interested in the subject, whether or not they have any church membership? This point is most important: for such a conference the aim is to have concerned, practising *doctors*. As Dr Eberhard Müller, the director of Bad Boll has written, 'We prepare our conferences not just together with other Christians, but if possible with various representatives of a certain group or profession, no matter what their faith may be. In an academy, the first step towards the preparation of a conference is a discussion between the Church and the secular world . . .

'We are very happy if the majority of participants at

a conference are non-church people. Non-church people don't speak openly if they feel they are in the minority and might be regarded as black sheep. They must feel that in an academy there is an atmosphere in which people can be open to each other.

'We have, therefore, never invited people through the local churches, but always try to find secular ways for an invitation. We put advertisements in the periodicals of different professional groups. We ask representatives of such secular organizations to sign the invitations (and we make a special effort to get people to sign who are not Protestants). Above all we ask participants of earlier conferences to bring their friends to the next conference. Over the years, the public has begun to know that people can come to an academy, not only if they are interested in religion but even more if they are interested in practical or intellectual questions.' (*Christian Comment*, No. 64, July 1965.)

It is far better to have two such groups in your experiment than four or five traditional church meetings; and it is of the utmost importance that such groups be involved in the planning and programme of their education, even if this means that some of the expectations of the leaders are not fulfilled at once, or even at all. This means a good deal of patient preparation for each group, and a good deal of informal meeting with lay people and *listening* to them. This is the hard graft of organizing new kinds of laity education : this is where naïve enthusiasm flags and impatient young theology students turn out to be failures—or show that they are possible leaders for the future. This is where a man must keep at things over a year or two, until he has the confidence and the backing of a reasonably wide circle of concerned laity. And this is what he must do, month after month, even when there is every temptation to rush impatiently after the latest gimmick or training centre.

For such a local experiment there are of course certain

minimum requirements in office equipment and in finance. If there is to be no special building, and meetings are to be held in private homes, in restaurants, in church rooms, or in pubs, then nevertheless there must be a certain efficiency and style in the arrangements, in the notepaper and printing, and in the whole operation. Lay people in the world rather expect the style of church work to be 'sloppy Gothic': they must be pleasantly surprised to find it different; and the finances should be adequate to cover incidental and secretarial expenses. In the United States, this is not such a problem. (And some of the experimenters there who think they are hardly done by do not know how fortunate they are with their typewriters and telephones and travel budgets. They are cramped financially for their programmes, but not grubbing around for postage stamps like some of their counterparts in Britain.) On our side of the Atlantic, it is even difficult to raise something like £200 for an experiment. But it is not impossible. Local churches and clergy are supposed to be in favour of the laity these days. Use a little ecumenical blackmail and ask for £10 each. Ask some of the concerned laity to squeeze their personal budgets a bit more, and give you £5 each (Billy Graham gets it for his style of laity education). Beg and bully and blackmail to collect the essential minimum of finance which will enable you to write to people and to get things started smartly and crisply. You will never regret it.

12. Large Public Events in Laity Education

As soon as cheap steamship and railway transport was available, the Church was presented with some new opportunities for lay education. There was now a chance of large national conferences and congresses, with membership drawn from a wide range of lay people from different regions of a country, and—more important—different countries of Europe and of the world.

Such chances were taken most eagerly in the United States, by British and European student Christian organizations, and by the world missionary societies. Their conference at Edinburgh in 1910 is considered by most church historians to mark the substantial beginnings of the modern ecumenical movement, which has certainly gratified travel agents, if not church leaders, ever since. Large international conferences, sometimes of a deliberative nature, sometimes of a deliberately cautious nature, are now common events in the world Church's calendars and expense accounts. They often have a vaguely educational flavour about them, particularly if a few captive laymen are allowed to be present. (Only the most churchy laity are likely to be able to attend, for all such conferences are overwhelmingly attended by top-brass clergy and church bureaucrats. Consider the delegations to the World Council of Churches general assemblies, such as Uppsala 1968.) It is also commonplace for such bodies as major American denominations, European student organizations, and so on, to bring together very considerable numbers of Christian people for some kind of educational experience.

Without doubt the most important and most con-

tinuous experiment of this kind has been the Germa..
Kirchentag,[1] founded by Dr Reinold von Thadden-Trieglaff after the Second World War and owing something
to the various Protestant conferences which had been
organized before the Hitler régime. Dr von Thadden also,
and deliberately, took note of the *organizational* efficiency of the great Nazi rallies of the 1930s; and, in his
bitter imprisonment in a Soviet prison camp in the
Arctic Circle, reflected on the possibility of the devil not
always having the best rallies.

The extraordinary story of Thadden's return to Germany and his foundation of the Kirchentag movement
has often been told: it is one of the greatest achievements of Christian laymen in our time. By 1950 he found
himself the leader of an enormous movement of adult
lay education, and it is still rather marvellous to con-
template the size and the efficiency of the early Kirchentags, held at a time when material resources were still
very short in post-war Germany. Certainly there has
never been anything else in the Church like the famous
Kirchentag held at Leipzig in 1954 in what was then the
Soviet Zone of Germany, with some 40,000 people
attending each day of lectures and Bible studies, and a
fantastic crowd, something like 700,000, at the final
open-air rally. The sheer diplomatic and organizational
skill required to obtain reluctant permission for such an
event, to arrange accommodation and food coupons and
press facilities and international visas and petrol sup-
plies, which all required constant haggling with both
East German and Soviet army authorities, was one of the
most remarkable feats in modern Christian history. And
the Kirchentags have continued every two years until
the present day (though, regrettably, never since 1954 in
the German Democratic Republic).

1. A *Kirchentag* is, literally, 'church day', but the post-war
series of German Kirchentags have been five-day events, from
Wednesday to Sunday.

Despite these successes, there is great suspicion among many Christian leaders about the value of such a massive and expensive event as an international congress or a Kirchentag. Not only in Britain but also in the United States there is real suspicion of religious 'rallies' and of the massing together of passive lay people to hear inspirational addresses from an archbishop or an evangelist. There have indeed sometimes been rather snide remarks suggesting that 'the Germans love to be on parade, after all' (it is worth emphasizing that the great crowds at a Kirchentag have always had a fine style of informal civilian discipline, like a London coronation crowd: they have never had anything much of a military flavour about them). Finally, and more seriously, critics of the Kirchentags and of similar experiments have often commented on the vagueness of the follow-up to such an event. 'What will be the results?' is always a good question to ask when a great deal of money is to be spent on Christian activities. In the case of an international congress they are always difficult to evaluate.

It is worth while spending a little time looking at the present style of Kirchentag (an organization with which one of the authors has been very considerably involved since 1954). It is, after all, one of the greatest experiments in lay education which the world Church has ever seen. And there still remains among Christian leaders and educators all over the world a very considerable ambivalence about this strangely persistent phenomenon. On the one hand, there are a good many critics of its style of operation (it is perhaps fair to say that some of them are basing their attitude on past Kirchentags, since in the nature of things few people outside Germany attend more than one or two of these giant events). On the other hand, there is a constant stream of Christian educators, especially from North America, who say with a certain gleam in their eyes, 'Surely we should have a

Kirchentag in Detroit, or Kansas City, or Vancouver, or London.'

We must stress, first of all, that the Kirchentags have moved on considerably from their early post-war style. There was—and the Kirchentag leadership always admitted this—a danger of fossilization by the end of the 1950s. The Kirchentags might have stuck in their early emphasis on problems of national rebirth and national unity which were, after all, the entirely natural pre-occupations of lay Christians in the bitter circumstances of post-war Germany (for example, the Kirchentag at Berlin in 1951 would have been horribly 'spiritual' and unrealistic if it had not concentrated largely on the controversial discussion of such topics). In some ways the Munich Kirchentag of 1959 and the Berlin Kirchentag of 1961[2] marked the end of the first type of Kirchentag. Since then, building very largely on Thadden's insights, and with his full encouragement, the Kirchentag leaders and committees have found a new style, and as Gerhard Schnath of their headquarters staff wrote in *Audenshaw Papers* (No. 4, December 1966):

'The Kirchentag has shaken itself out of its proven and traditional ways ... The Kirchentag is now again openly, controversially, excitingly engaged in relating our Christian faith to the problems of 1967 and 1984, and not trying to console people for the tragic difficulties of 1945 or 1950. I believe we have found a new flexibility, and a readiness to experiment and to take risks.'

Here, in summary, are the marks of a modern German Kirchentag. We would suggest, with respect, that anyone thinking of organizing a similar event in North America or elsewhere (and this is perfectly possible) should note them with care, with prayer, and with courage.

2. Held just, only just, before the building of the Wall: the original date for the last Kirchentag service – Thadden's seventieth birthday – was in fact the Sunday that the world woke to learn that the Wall had been erected.

1. A Kirchentag remains a major public event. It deserves and expects major attention from national and civic leadership and from the TV, the press, and the mass media generally. It will certainly stop the traffic more than once; and it will provide at least one or two news stories involving major public figures. If the secular world is to be invited to attend, in the persons of notable government and industrial figures, and to devote time on millions of little screens to critical coverage of the congress, then it must be worth such attention. The Kirchentag style is not that of a Baptist hymn-sing in Oklahoma City, nor that of a missionary rally in Westminster Abbey. The style of worship, of speakers, and of education must be appropriate for such a major public *open* occasion. It is always important to remember how many people attend a Kirchentag who have not been seen in their local church for years.

2. Despite, or indeed because of, this public and open nature of a Kirchentag, a style of Christian controversy must be built into the whole programme, both into the daily Bible studies and into the other lectures and arguments. This is where a Kirchentag is so different from a eucharistic congress or an evangelistic meeting. It is in no sense an emotionally comforting rally of the faithful or a conditioning of passive listeners. It is a massive and challenging public confrontation of Christians and non-Christians alike about the main areas of human responsibility today. For instance, the lectures at the Hanover Kirchentag in 1967 included such topics as the political problems of peace-making today, and the urgent need for reform of the institutional churches and there was bitter debate about many of these. At Stuttgart in 1969 there were demonstrations and fierce arguments about church reform and about German aid to the developing countries.

The Kirchentag organizers are constantly struggling with the problems of discussion groups in such a large assembly. At Dortmund in 1963 it was possible to have several hundred smallish groups (about fifty or so) all looking at the same open-ended films each morning. This was reasonably successful, but appallingly expensive. At Cologne in 1965 and Hanover in 1967 there were experiments in the use of TV channels in the same way. The international centre at each Kirchentag has—ever since Munich 1959—managed to offer really small discussion groups, and British and American participants have helped enormously in the development of this tradition. But whether there is official organization of small groups or not, the Kirchentag programme allows for many informal groups to develop, often around light refreshments, at intervals in the daily programme (for only a religious maniac attempts to take in all the events arranged during the week). Such Christian controversy involves everybody, from a cabinet minister downwards, simply because very many of the concerns of the laity today are controversial. There are no simple answers; there is no Christian 'party line'.

It would not be different for an American or indeed an African Kirchentag. Some of those who have longed for a massive event, say in Chicago or Los Angeles, do not always seem to have appreciated that the main topics of a Kirchentag in the United States today would have to be—quite inevitably—American foreign policy, Black Power, the gap between the generations, and the bitter differences between the rich nations and the poor ones. There would also be more than a comment or two about the sickness of the Church if not on the presumed death of God. These sorts of topics are constantly prominent at the German Kirchentags, and that is one reason why you can find so many non-church members and so many younger people at them.

3. Moreover, such a style of controversy must not be 'cooked'. We have had enough examples of phoney Christian dialogue, with everybody coming finally to an

orthodox conclusion in time for the blessing. Some of the
major speakers must be asked to give their honest
opinions without being required to sign the Apostles'
Creed in advance. And participation in the Kirchentag
must be completely open, with enrolment possible and
indeed encouraged through non-church channels. A Kirchentag recruited entirely through the denominational
networks, with parish ministers organizing bus parties
and the choir given the evening off, a Kirchentag made
up almost exclusively of good loyal church members, is
no Kirchentag. Of course, a good many people come
with the support and encouragement of church authorities, but a good many find their way to the lectures and
discussion groups much more unofficially and even
anonymously. And in recent years, by no means all the
parish ministers have been unanimous in support of the
radicalism of the Kirchentag. It may even be surmised
that the attempted boycott of the Hanover Kirchentag
by the 'No other Gospel' movement in 1967 was a distinct help in encouraging some of the less old-fashioned
lay people and students to attend!

Such an openness to the world and to non-church
people would be familiar enough to some student leaders
in Britain and in North America, but it would disturb
some of the more traditional church bureaucrats, and
maybe their sources of financial support.

4. Any Kirchentag must be extremely ecumenical in
its outlook. Thadden wished this from the start, for he
comes from a family tradition of European involvement
and learnt his international Christianity from the World
Student Christian Federation before the dark days of the
Nazis. Indeed, from the first proper Kirchentag at Essen
in 1950 he bullied the ecumenical establishment of those
days into active and time-consuming support of the congresses—dumbfounding Visser 't Hooft, Franklin Clark
Fry, and the others by the astounding success of the first
meetings. This was not merely because, most wisely, he

wanted the Kirchentag to help educate German Christians in the world and the world Church outside their own unhappy country. It was also because he saw, as usual earlier and more sharply than most people, that the new ecumenical movement must be more than international committees of bishops and church treasurers. He was always insistent that the Kirchentag must spend time and money organizing a considerable international delegation to each congress, and skilfully enlisted the American Methodist Dr Franklin H. Littell as the first and most energetic chairman of a permanent Kirchentag ecumenical committee. Dr Richard von Weizsäcker, the present president of the Kirchentag, and the small and overworked permanent headquarters staff have faithfully and enthusiastically continued this tradition; and there are normally something between 800 and 1,000 international and ecumenical participants in a Kirchentag. They are a great expense, and a great nuisance to organize; and they are very welcome. For they bring an indispensable element of international concern and experience into the meetings.

Inside Germany, the ecumenical problem is both simpler and sometimes more intractable. The smaller Protestant churches join quite enthusiastically in each Kirchentag, and are represented on the various organizing committees. For many years, Catholics have been asked to offer hospitality in their homes for Protestants attending a Kirchentag (the Protestants do the same if there is a Katholikentag). Ever since the Dortmund Kirchentag in 1963 there has been very great sympathy with the principles of the Kirchentag on the part of many high Roman Catholic leaders, and Catholics have been strenuously encouraged to attend the Kirchentag meetings. This is a wonderful example of interdenominational friendship, and has gone far beyond formal gestures of goodwill. Perhaps the highlight of this new approval of the work of the Kirchentag was the congress in the great Catholic city of Cologne in 1965, where the Cardinal Archbishop held a formal reception for the Kirchentag leaders. And now there are plans for a jointly sponsored Catholic and Protestant assembly at Augsburg in 1971. There are still some problems ahead, which are not unrelated to the styles of discussion and open controversy that may be expected.

5. A Kirchentag must be organized with superb efficiency. And this is an important matter to stress, and a difficult thing for Christian people to achieve. Kirchentag organization has to be first class because the education and indeed the convenience and comfort of so many people are involved, and because the eyes of the world are upon you. You have offered to be, as it were, host to thousands of people (who may have had disappointing experiences of church hospitality and church organization in the past). You must not let them down. Your efficiency has to be first class, to the point of not being noticed. There must be provision for emergencies— many special 'phones, reserve projectors, extra chairs, walkie-talkies, and so on but there must not be an atmosphere of crisis, nor (except perhaps for the final open-air rally) any great sense of being organized. The efficiency must be good enough to be unobserved and taken for granted by most of the participants.

Such organization is certainly within human capabilities nowadays, and this is another example of the right use of modern skills and technologies. But it requires a good deal of money and a great deal of disciplined and efficient voluntary work months before and weeks after a Kirchentag. When the Hanover Kirchentag opened in July 1967, some twenty-five committees had been working for twelve months beforehand, some 700 volunteers had been enrolled, and housewives had registered to take, without charge, some 15,000 visitors for bed and breakfast. Here undoubtedly German dutifulness has worked for the success of the Kirchentag. Very many people complain that it is difficult to get voluntary workers these days (and many of these housewives, for instance, were going out to work as well as running a home and family). It is even more common to find complaints that people will not stick at voluntary jobs after a few weeks. There are plenty of minor crises and grumbles in Kirchentag committees during the long weeks before the congress opens; but the general standard of dedication and efficiency is wonderfully high.

Even with all this voluntary labour, there are still heavy expenses. The German Kirchentag is financed by a very skilful blend of personal, city, and church contributions, so that it remains unbound to any source of funds. This is another tribute to Thadden's wisdom and skill in the early days: he might easily have come under obligations to either church or state sources of support. Now, though from time to time there are financial crises, it is perhaps less easy to let the Kirchentag down; and both church and civic leaders have provided financial help with little more than the expected grumbles. It is worth remarking how the Protestant church authorities have been prepared, without too much fuss, to support from their massive church funds an organization which has always insisted on its formal independence from the *Evangelische Kirche in Deutschland*, and which has been a major forum for criticism of the organized churches. Perhaps some of them are glad to see such a forum exists, for which they are not themselves responsible.

There is no doubt that such financial requirements would be extremely difficult to meet in Britain today (and this is one of the reasons for the struggles of the Scottish Kirk Week organization). They are entirely within the reach of American churches, who have substantial denominational funds, and also the possibility of extraordinary generosity on the part of private donors. It is rather disappointing that a good many American educators have talked generally about having a Kirchentag experiment in the USA, and have then backed away when they realized, not so much the financial but more the controversial nature of a true Kirchentag. It would be enormously valuable to try an American experiment, as a possible model for lay education in the future. But it would require high religious, political, and financial courage.

13. The Education of Christian Revolutionaries

There is no doubt that the 1970s will be a period in which different styles of revolutionary politics will be suggested as appropriate solutions to the world's deep and persistent injustices. This is of course particularly the case in some countries of Latin America, and in the United States, where the beastly miseries of the inner-city ghettos, the seemingly permanent bias of white society against black and Indian people, and the failure of many proposed 'liberal' policies are combining to drive many people to violent policies of despair and anger.

Christian people certainly cannot escape involvement in such desperate matters, and if any church or denomination tries, it will merely make itself ridiculous, especially in the eyes of the young. For several years now (notably at the Church and Society conference of the World Council of Churches in Geneva in 1966, and at various meetings of the World Student Christian Federation), intelligent and responsible leaders from Latin America and elsewhere have been trying to educate the mild and respectably liberal leaders of European churches about the tragic institutional repression and violence of many régimes in the modern world. Those North American Christians who have been involved in inner-city work and in problems of rural poverty and injustice have been speaking strangely violent words at committees of their denominations or of the National Council of Churches. And Mr James Forman's Black Manifesto in 1969 certainly introduced a bitter flavour of revolutionary rhetoric to many of the summer conferences and conventions of that year.

It is therefore urgently necessary that schemes for laity education should include some careful and intelligent study of revolutionary politics, and of the involvement of Christians in such drastic attempts to shift power in modern society. It must be admitted that many so-called 'Christian revolutionaries'—especially in the United States—have stumbled sincerely, even passionately, into rhetorical and political positions which they imperfectly understand, and which their traditional Christian or secular education has not helped them to understand. Here two blocks to our common understanding of the position have been serious. In the first place, many eager Christian radicals—especially perhaps theological students—have almost no idea of the development of secular radicalism and revolutionary thinking over the past two hundred years—the growth of Marxism in all its varieties, the different theories of anarchism, and the development of fascism and totalitarianism. Such matters are commonplaces of many history and political science courses, but not perhaps in theological seminaries, especially in America. And second, there is an understandable but very serious gap between the political thinking of almost all Americans (except refugees of the 1930s and later) and almost all Europeans. The United States had its major revolution a long time ago—in 1766—and its civil war in 1865. Since then they have, blessedly, escaped massive violence within their continental boundaries. No bombs have destroyed New York or St Louis or Los Angeles as they have destroyed Warsaw or Hamburg. No armies have made Omaha or Pittsburg a desert as in Amiens or Berlin or Stalingrad. American justice is often uncertain, and their prisons cruel and insanitary, but they have had no Dachau, nor work camps in Alaska like the horrors of the Arctic Circle penitentiaries in the Soviet Union. Nor have the libraries of Harvard and Berkeley been purged and 'unsuitable' volumes destroyed as in the burning of

the books in Germany in 1933. If we are to talk of revolutionary politics, all this kind of violence is on the
agenda, and part of the terrible price we may have to
pay. Christians who wish to enter into revolutionary
activities ought to know what they are about.

We refer in our Bibliography to a number of secular
books which may be of great help in such studies. In this
chapter we can only try to offer some general classification of revolutionary theories which may help our
readers to sort things out, and to understand the tragic
richness of experience in violence and revolution which
man has achieved in the last two hundred years of his
history.

Those who desire radical change in human society
can, in general, be sorted out into three main categories,
according to the overreaching goals which they set
themselves:

A. Those who are determined to establish and organize
a just and humane society for all mankind—for all
human beings, regardless of race, class, sex, intelligence,
or anything else.

B. Those who are determined to establish and organize
a just and humane society for 'our people'—for certain
(probably oppressed) categories of human beings, maybe
the proletariat, the blacks, the young, the Jews, the
Catholics, and so on.

C. *Those who do not wish any organized society at all*,
in any style that we now have, but who wish to abolish
all the present structures of society (except perhaps the
family and the local village or settlement) because they
maintain that a truly free and humane life depends on
liberation from social structures. These are properly
called *anarchists*. The name is often used as a term of
abuse, but Christians should know better. The long and
involved history of different styles of anarchistic theory
—both secular and Christian—demands much time.
patience, and sympathy.

Revolutionaries may also be classified according to the methods which they are prepared to adopt to reach goals A, B, and C above.

1. Some revolutionaries are *utopians*. They either have wildly perfectionist schemes for social change, which frankly nobody can reasonably adopt, or they decide to try to start a new and pure and idealistic community away from the sordid confusion of present cities and societies. Such attempts have been a part of the vision and dreams of mankind throughout the centuries (and notably in the nineteenth century when many such experiments were started in the United States); but none have lasted—at least in their original forms.

2. Many who have desired genuinely radical changes in society have been what may be called *constitutional radicals*. They have believed that the democratic process existing in a country like Britain, or the United States, or Denmark, may (no doubt with continual reform of things like electoral laws and the legal rights of minorities) produce not merely minor and token concessions to the poor and the oppressed but major and radical changes and a drastically improved social order. Such opinions are often mocked in radical circles at the moment, and any concessions by, for instance, the US administration or the Congress or the Swedish government are sneered at as 'repressive toleration', 'liberal tokenism'.

We must insist that before radicals dismiss as useless the democratic processes which have been developed (notably in Britain and the United States) in the last two hundred years, they consider very carefully indeed what has been achieved by such constitutional methods, and also the price they—and we—must pay if such methods of social change are discarded. It is simply not right to suggest that constitutional governments always and only produce slow, minor, evolutionary changes in society, though no doubt sometimes this is all their sluggish pro-

cedures can achieve. It is, however, evident that sometimes in human affairs men have found the established
procedures so fossilized and so dominated by power
blocs or vested interests of some kind or another, that
they have felt that they must resort to armed force and
more drastic methods of change.

3. Many radicals have been *pacifists* of one kind or
another, and have insisted that change must be achieved
by *non-violent means*. They have been prepared to use
moral power against a monarch or dictator or slow-mov-
ing parliament: they have often been prepared to use
non-violent forms of protest and, indeed, to make public
nuisances of themselves, disrupting public affairs or the
traffic in order to force both the government and the
general public to note their arguments. Mahatma Ghandi
and Martin Luther King are only two of the most distinguished proponents of these theories in recent times.

It must be noted that such methods of non-violent
protest depend for their success (in as much as success is
looked for by pacifists at all) very largely on the moral
principles held by the people in power. When Ghandi's
women supporters lay down in the road in an Indian
city, their protest was rather effective; for no British
commander could decently order cars or tanks to pro-
ceed over their frail and defenceless bodies. It is not clear
that such methods would have deterred either Nazi or
Japanese commanders in the last world war. Some pacifists will immediately insist that, nevertheless, the total
repudiation of force is called for by Christian or other
religious principles; and we would respect their convictions without here following their deep and passionate
arguments further. Other radicals will (as in recent years
in the United States, both before and after the murder of
Martin Luther King) move from non-violent to more
aggressive styles of protest.

4. Some will adopt a policy of *reluctant revolution*. In
the last resort, and after all methods of democratic pro-

cess and peaceful change have been tried, they will say, 'There is nothing for it but armed revolution.' It is certainly not for British or American or French citizens to suggest that revolution is inevitably wrong or useless. The events of 1688, of 1776, and of 1789 are not unimportant in history. Indeed the whole tone and contents of the American Declaration of Independence are a classic example of the arguments of reluctant revolutionaries. They would have liked to come to reasonable terms with George III and his British ministers. They regret very much that they cannot. But, in the last resort, they claim their right to revolt.

Similar arguments have been put forward in our day by radicals in Latin America, and by resistance movements in Germany, the Netherlands, France, and in Czechoslovakia. When Dietrich Bonhoeffer accepted the opportunity to join in the underground plots against Hitler, it was after much agonizing and reluctance; but he did it. And thousands of good decent people in Europe have in the last thirty years reluctantly and painfully, but also grimly and determinedly, done dreadful things to destroy tyranny. But they have done them reluctantly; and they have hoped for a time when they would no longer be necessary.

5. Other radicals have become what can only be called *fervent and enthusiastic revolutionaries*. They have adopted violent methods, not with distaste and as a last resort, but willingly and wholeheartedly as the only appropriate historical methods to enforce change. They are convinced that any other methods—constitutional radicalism, non-violence, and so on—are only trivial attempts to cope with the deep-seated evils of society and the institutional and violent repression organized by the people now in power. Such wholehearted endorsement of violence is a terrible development of political theory since the eighteenth century. Its most appalling results have been the ghastly régimes of fascists and

Nazis in Europe up to 1945 : an exaltation of violence to gain total supremacy for one 'race'—the so-called Aryan people. Little less terrible has been the advocacy of the class war by Marx and Lenin and Stalin, and in particular that horrible extension of communist violence by Stalin which led both to the insane purges of Russians in the 1930s and in the 1940s, and to the terrible persecutions in Poland and in the Baltic States in 1939–40. Present-day enthusiastic revolutionaries—like the Students for a Democratic Society—are not perhaps so clear as to the extent of the violence which they will use, nor as to the goals which they hope to achieve—whether communist, anarchist, or what have you. They should at least understand the political heritage which they are adopting, and the dangers which they run.

We would suggest that any attempt nowadays at laity education must include some serious and sympathetic consideration of the different goals and styles of revolution which we have listed summarily above. We suggest also that it will not be enough to give such a tidy analysis, in the rather bloodless style of some civics and political science classes. Here, above all, neutrality is not enough; and young Christians in particular will expect their educators to have the nerve and the guts to enter this basic controversy of our times.

In our opinion, Christian revolutionaries can properly only adopt *goal A* above—the organization of a just and humane society for *all mankind*, regardless of race, class, religion, sex, etc. And they must struggle to choose between methods :

2—constitutional radicalism,

3—non-violent revolution,

and

4—reluctantly violent revolution.

They should try to reject :

goal B—a just and humane society for only 'our

people' (whether they be white, black, middle-class, Christian, northern European, or anything else),

goal C—the abolition of all organized society,

method 1—the utopian solution,

and

method 5—enthusiastic and fervent revolution.

We make no apologies for emphasizing the words 'struggle' and 'try' in these comments, for two reasons. Observers and analysts of revolutions often forget that they are witnessing and reporting historical events of great power, which very few human beings can in any sense pretend to control. A revolution is not always a liberating experience for those caught in it: you often find that it limits the choices you can realistically make. In the second place, the possibilities of constructive revolution in some parts of the world today are desperately slim. In such circumstances, there may be an obligation to 'prophesy'—to take a stand despite its probably horrible effects for you and your family and colleagues, and despite the fact that an efficient totalitarian régime will do its beastly best to ensure that your prophesying is not heard or noticed. There may be an obligation to wait patiently and prayerfully for a better time for revolution. And no outsider can judge for you.

Presumably most of our readers will agree without question that goal B—justice only for 'our people'—is an inadequate one if Christ Jesus died for all men, and not just for white Protestants or for British citizens. We must note, however, that very many idealistic revolutionary movements are soon corrupted by such partial visions: and indeed many of the most powerful movements in history—Jewish nationalism, Roman imperialism, American Protestantism—have thrived precisely because they have had an 'enemy', a despised race or nation or class of outsiders who were not 'saved', or 'civilized', or worthy of God or man's respect. It is still

very difficult for English or German Christians to consider 'funny', 'scruffy', 'simple' Africans or Asians as
fellow human beings. It is appallingly difficult for angry
Brazilian peasants or American Black Panthers to think
of a society in which both they and their oppressors will
have a common humanity and dignity. But this is what
the New Testament calls us to. We cannot settle for less.
In the Gospel there are no outsiders.

We cannot deal here with all the age-long arguments
among Christians as to goal C (a structureless society)
and method 1 (the utopian solution), although it is not
really fair to brush aside such traditions in human thinking without more careful consideration than we can give
in this summary. Most Christian writers have suggested
that the founders of new societies and communes have
not wrestled hard enough with the fact of sin in the
world, and with the complex mixture of individual and
social glory and wickedness which appears in all human
societies, even the most idealistic. Nor can we deal
adequately with the agonizing arguments which are now
engaging and even disrupting many churches as to the
methods 2, 3, 4, and 5 which we have outlined above.
But in this case, we must at least try to suggest some
profitable lines of controversy.

Firstly, at the risk of being considered mild, old-
fashioned 'liberal' moderates, we wish to insist with great
emphasis that it simply is not true that in all countries
and in all situations the resources of constitutional radicalism (method 2 above) are exhausted. The fruits of
centuries of Western struggling towards a constitutional
and democratic society are not so lightly to be despised
or discarded, whether it be the procedures of reform in
Britain, the rights of free speech in a European university
(including the rights of unpopular minorities to be heard
without disruption of their meetings) or the simple protection of all peaceful citizens from arbitrary arrest and
imprisonment. It is true that politics in Britain may seem

at times to be rather mediocre and flat, but we do well to remember that the Churchill government of 1940 and the Attlee government of 1945 both succeeded in much radical and effective action without destroying the liberties of ordinary citizens. We would do well to recall the extraordinary social achievements of, for instance, the democratic governments of New Zealand and of Sweden. It is very understandable that radicals in the United States feel at the moment great frustration at the slow pace of social change in their country, and a kind of sick fury at the assassination of J. F. Kennedy, Martin Luther King, and their most promising constitutional radical— R. F. Kennedy. Yet there is certainly as yet no evidence that these murders were part of a political plot to stop social change; and if Robert Kennedy had not been shot, and if he had been elected president (which is by no means inconceivable) then hopes of constitutional but impressive change might very well be totally different from what they are now. And it is not likely that radical political talent in a country the size of the United States resides solely in the members of one great and tragic family.

Partly because of the great price to be paid once men resort to violence, it is surely a duty of Christians to try as hard as they possibly can to use constitutional and peaceful and non-violent means to bring about change. But there may be times—there certainly have been times —when Christians have felt that they had to agree to method 4 (reluctant revolution). We cannot accept that they should accept any style of revolution which may be considered method 5 (enthusiastic revolution).

This needs to be said bluntly, for the naïve way in which a few Christians—especially in the United States —have joyfully endorsed the most violent policies of extreme revolution has been most unhelpful, and is suspect psychologically, pragmatically, and theologically. There have been a certain number of white middle-class mini-

sters going round saying almost gleefully, 'After all, violence is as American as cherry pie.' This is quite dreadful.
Of course, in some sense violence is as human as original
sin, and lust, and hate, and anger; but it is one great test
of a civilized country how *little* you resort to violence,
even in dealing with violent opponents. And how clearly
you understand that violence breeds violence, in you and
in your opponents, from arguments and pamphlets to
street fights and riots all the terrible way to Dachau and
Treblinka. Some people in America are so eager to call
their disturbed country 'fascist'. Do they really have any
understanding of what a fascist régime is really like? For
instance, the Chicago riots and police repression at the
time of the Democratic convention in 1968 was of
course a disgrace to a great city and to a great country,
but how many demonstrators were actually tortured to
death, or even killed? How many are now languishing in
concentration camps in northern Alaska? How many
have had their ashes delivered by registered post to their
fearful relations? Of course there is great injustice in the
United States and there is much hidden and institutional
violence in the repression of southern blacks, and the
inner-city poor and Indians on the reservations. But this
will not be changed by exaggerating the fascism in
American life, or by indulging in the heady joys of revolutionary hate jargon. It is exhilarating fun, but it is not
in any true sense genuinely liberating to chant '—you
fascist pigs' at police or legislators or university admini-
strators.

Nor is it at all certain to achieve very much. One
reason why Christians have to accept a resort to violence
reluctantly and carefully and with much heart searching
is that they have to try to work out whether a revolution is likely to succeed or not. For instance, it is clear
that while Martin Luther King's methods did achieve
major successes for the blacks (successes which of course
left much still undone but which transformed the legal

position for many Negroes), the confrontation tactics of recent months have produced a most powerful 'white backlash' which makes further progress for blacks or other minorities much less certain. It is necessary to be grimly realistic here—as Lenin was years ago in his pamphlet, *'Left-Wing' Communism*. Because of modern police and government technology, armed insurrection or any attempt to disrupt city life by means of strikes, sabotage, and so on is very much less likely to succeed than in the last century. 1848 saw the end of simple popular insurrections. A valuable book by Martin Oppenheimer, *The Urban Guerilla*, has pointed this out with admirable clarity—it is one of the few American books on revolution to draw widely on European experience.

This is not, we repeat, not, to say that Christians will never feel it necessary to take to armed revolution. It is to say that they must try to count the cost. A British student leader reported some months ago (in *Student World*, Summer, 1969 issue) that he had been asked for advice by some Rhodesian students, who felt that their country was becoming so repressive and totalitarian that they must resort to drastic remedies. Similar agonizing goes on all the time among young Christians in South Africa, in Brazil, and in some countries of central Europe : and they are not theoretical drawing-room or coffee-house discussions.

Wisely, the British leader insisted that in the last resort only the Rhodesian students themselves could decide. (How easy it is for Christians who live in safety to offer advice to those in the front line of political and revolutionary involvement.) But he did offer three criteria by which perhaps they might be helped to a decision :

1. *Have all the alternatives to violence been exhausted?*

2. *Will you use as little violence as possible in achieving your revolution?* If you blow up a train, what of the

innocent who are killed? If you organize a riot, how many will be arrested and shot? Remember how many of those who suffer in a ghetto riot are poor blacks. And the 'enemy' are also your fellow human beings.

3. *Will the revolution have any chance of success?*

We would like to suggest, in conclusion, that both historical analysis and recent experience shows four qualities which can distinguish the true Christian revolutionary from the false. In the first place, he will have a very strong personal discipline. Here the communists have much to teach us. Year by year, long before they came to power anywhere, they developed a persistent veteran efficiency which puts so many Christians to shame. Paul Goodman once wrote 'student protest evaporates with the summer vacation'; and it is not different for many young Christian radicals. Where are the fervent protesters of five years ago? How can Christians learn to persist in a radical and effective stance, year after year? Here our comments on the need for an intelligent and self-critical fellowship of support for innovators are perhaps especially relevant (see p. 123).

Second: a Christian revolutionary must have some sense of humour. Psychologically, radical types tend of course to be puritan, humourless, fanatical types: like the revolutionary leader in the armoured train in *Dr Zhivago*. But, as Jürgen Moltmann has written, 'I would hope that Christians, who believe in God's presence in the midst of the revolution, would be able to laugh and sing and dance like the firstborn of all creation. . . . They are perhaps the fools of the revolution—those who love it but who also laugh about it and shock people.'

Third: a Christian revolutionary will hold calmly and persistently to the doctrine of hope. (As Dr Moltmann has also noticeably insisted.) We have met in recent months too many Christian radicals who are wallowing in despair, and guilt and gloom. This is not a proper

Christian repentance about the past: it is a bitter hope-lessness which erodes all constructive plans for the future. This is psychologically self-destructive and theo-logically idiotic. Christians are not a people without hope.

And fourth: despite all the tragedy of oppression and violence which he must feel for his own people if not for himself, a Christian radical will somehow, by faith if not yet by experience, hold to the doctrine of love and jus-tice for *all men*, not just for his side. This is a preacher's cliché, a lecturer's theory; and how can a man in a Brazilian prison or an Alabama woman with a starving baby say 'Yes' to it? But this is the Gospel; and, wonder-fully, in the middle of war or revolution or imprison-ment or brainwashing God has enabled his people to love their enemies. It will be so in our times too.

14. The Way Forward

We have tried in this book to say something about the vocation of God's people in tomorrow's world and something about the styles of education which they may find helpful. It would be pleasant to end there; but it would be wrong. For when adults are educated in the general attitudes suggested in this book and in *God's Frozen People*, and when they are committed to carrying their Christian faith into the controversial areas of human life today and tomorrow, then they will often feel that the institutional churches, far from supporting them, actually try to hold them back. And if we are serious about encouraging a new style of Christian life and witness, we must be honest enough to think about what will happen to the laity once they are committed in this new way, and to face very frankly the tensions which may arise between them and less radical church members.

Hans Jochum Margull put it very bluntly in an article for *Christian Comment* (No 53): 'Our congregations in Europe demand from every new member not only a conversion but also a change in culture. He has to abandon some of his contemporary behaviour, and to accept the older patterns prevalent among the majority of the congregation. The new Christian has to learn the old hymns and to appreciate them. He has to learn the language of the pulpit. He has to share in some conservative political opinions. He has to dress a bit old-fashioned. He has to learn how to take part in a congregation in which there is no discussion. In brief, he has to step back two generations and undergo what one may call a painful cultural circumcision.'

We suspect that many younger and more radical Christians in North America might indeed insist that there is more than two generations' difference between the cultural patterns of Harvard Square and Telegraph Avenue, of Berkeley and a small town congregation in Iowa or New Jersey.

It is also clear that many of the hopes in Britain, in Europe, and in North America about a renewal of the laity have come to nothing. Despite the writing and teaching of Hendrick Kraemer, Hans-Ruedi Weber, Franklin Littell, and other distinguished teachers in the lay movement, many lay people have been unable to hold together a live membership of the Church and a genuine involvement in the affairs of the world. Some of them, especially in Britain, have finally lost hope in the institutional churches; those left now in the pews are often very churchy laity who are as ecclesiastical as any archdeacon. Of course we have had some successes over the years—some work on Iona, at Dunblane and Teesside, some good parish study courses, some valuable new skills in small group work, some promising specialist discussions on subjects such as religion and medicine. But if we are to be honest, we have to admit that so far these have all had a very modest impact on the churches and on British society in general.

In the United States church congregations are by no means as diminished as in Britain and in Europe, and at first sight they are far less dominated by the over-fifties. Nevertheless, in many local churches those—young or old—who wish to innovate in matters of church or society often find themselves unwelcome or uncomfortable. A great deal of North American church life is in fact organized—or at least quietly controlled—by responsible, solid, conservative citizens who hold responsible, solid, middle-class jobs or have fairly recently retired from them. This means that the churches are always in serious danger of becoming the psychological refuges of people who are disturbed and unhappy about the pace of change in the modern world outside, and who look to their local church as the one thing which does not change. The one static certainty in an unpleasantly uncertain future. The hymns that bring back memories. The slightly rigorous, very secure ritual of Sunday morning church parade, where unorthodox opinions (from the pulpit or from fellow worshippers) are as suspect as over-long hair.

We must probe deeper here, though it may hurt. We must try to spell out some of the causes for bitterness and distress and even anger which make it so difficult for radical Christians seeking a relevant Church to find it round the corner. For instance, many of our differences about worship today, in both Catholic and Protestant churches, are due to differences in cultural and theological outlook between the generations. What older church members like is a familiar service, a supportive ritual. This is also what occasional visitors to churches often expect and like—soaring choirs, obscure and dignified language, a 'holy' feeling, a grand white wedding, a good dose of impressive religiosity. But more innovative people want the services to mean something, to connect theologically with today and tomorrow rather than the Middle Ages or the nineteenth century. And when they start to think about the services they are asked to attend, they at once raise some difficulties which more traditional people have simply never articulated before.

As Dorothea Sölle said in her famous talk to the Cologne Kirchentag in 1965: 'There is in our modern world less and less traditional religion. We cannot reverse this process. We can no longer take for granted all these things which once defined the Christian life—saying grace at meals, going to church on Sundays, and so on. ... I would like to accept all these standards if I could —but all this is impossible for me. It doesn't work any more. Doubt and scepticism, rationality and self-consciousness: these are the ingredients of the air we breathe. Why should the parson, or the Bible, or religious custom, or traditional worship be exempt?'

Many lay people today are very unhappy about both the language and the style of local church services. They do not normally want slang or the temporary jargon of hit songs; and they are quite prepared to accept something of the 'mystery' and awe of Christian worship. They are not, however, happy to address the Lord as if he were an oriental despot with very little sense of fairness or even consistency, or as if he had special favourites like the English or the Americans. They do not see why so many Sunday services have to be exercises in clerical monologue. They simply cannot accept that the Holy Communion should still so often be the symbol of our *disunity* in Christ.

More than this, their understanding about the real purpose of the Church as the embodiment of Christ's love for his world—is such that they find local congregations far too self-centred and concerned only with 'our kind of people'. They find it basically unchristian when Sunday worship can take place without a conscientious agonizing over—and even sometimes a celebration of—the life of the world outside. And they find it simply indecent when prayers and intercessions are offered Sunday by Sunday without specific reference to such tragedies as the war in Vietnam.

Martin Luther King Jr wrote, in his famous letter from the Birmingham jail, in 1963: 'The judgement of God is upon the Church as never before. If the Church of today does not recapture the sacrificial spirit of the early Church, it will lose its authentic ring, forfeit the loyalty of millions, and be dismissed as an irrelevant social club with no meaning for the twentieth century. I am meeting young people every day whose disappointment with the Church has risen to outright disgust.'

The net result is, for very many church people (and not only young ones), that they make a quiet decision : 'Jesus Christ, *yes*; the Church, *no*.' They are not pagans, and it is offensively inaccurate to call them such. They wish to keep some standards of Christian living : they intend to bring up their children in a living faith; they often continue to pray regularly. But, except for major ritual occasions in life : 'The Church, *no*.'

Such drop-outs do not normally make a fuss. They leave church membership quietly, a little shamefacedly, perhaps when they go off to college, or change their job, or start night work. And this is seemly, for it is not considered proper to upset people in the Church, that cosy society in which the bland lead the bland. We have seen this process happen in Britain year after year, especially in the industrial areas such as London and Manchester and Glasgow. The more lively young people seem to go first. And now there are perceptible signs that the same phenomenon is happening in at least the urban areas of the United States and Canada.

Among students, such a drift from church membership is now so commonplace that many church leaders even take it as inevitable. 'They will come back later' is what is often said. Perhaps they may—when they settle in a pleasant suburb, and the children grow up and ought to go to church school, and the mother, at least, feels a bit guilty and uneasy. Or even later, when there is a need for quiet companionship in the dull afternoons, or there is long sickness, or loneliness, or retirement. Such a late renewal of church membership may be a fine thing; but it may be (especially for the men) only a domestic and leisure-time and partial matter. So often the major decisions of life have been made, or go on being made, without any reference to Christian teaching or commitment, because in the crucial years of early adulthood there has been no assessment of the style of life aimed at, the careers designed, the income and responsibilities enjoyed. To come back later is to return much less free than you went.

'Then we must have a radically new kind of church.' This is often said nowadays, sometimes rather wildly and desperately, sometimes rather quietly and hesitantly, as if it were wrong to come to this conclusion. And in one sense this can be a dreadful suggestion. If the Church of Jesus Christ is to be split once more, not by denominations but by age groups or social attitudes or styles of worship, then we shall face new miseries. Some of those who talk rather easily about a new reformation seem to miss the deep tragedy of the last one. But we must recognize that if old and young, radicals and conservatives, are to be held—even loosely—in one institutional structure, then there will have to be very major changes. Many of the laity, and a good many of the clergy, are not going to put up any longer with things as they are.

In the first place, critical members of a local church must have a chance—and must recognize it as their duty —to speak out frankly and courteously in love, and not just slide away quietly because open controversy is embarrassing. (This applies just as much to critical members who are conservative and who sometimes withdraw their membership and their financial support without ever explaining why.) Young adults, especially, must be given more than a nominal opportunity to discuss things. Their opinions must be given something like the weight offered to the over-fifties. It must be recognized that they are full and responsible church members, entirely entitled not only to have a youth service once a year but to have their opinions seriously considered. Let them at eighteen have full adult rights (and responsibilities) in the churches as in the nation. And let there be real hesitation before anyone mutters 'heresy' or, even worse, 'disloyalty' under his breath. True loyalty to one's country and one's church means frank, responsible criticism sometimes, not pretending all is well when it isn't.

We are convinced that a second essential for most institutional churches in the future is to recognize that a proper hunger for Christian unity does not, thank God, require a dull uniformity in Christian organization and worship and education. Christians have begun to recognize that a Catholic mass and a Quaker silence may be both pleasing to God and psychologically appropriate for the people taking part. We shall all have to accept a similar pluralism in very many other ways, not only denominationally but for different national and regional cultures and for different types and ages of worshippers. There must be no hidden tokenism here, suggesting that an occasional pop service or African meditation may be permitted, but that something like *The Book of Common Prayer* is really the norm, the divinely appointed 'right way' to do things. And the same plurality must be accepted for many kinds of church organization. The village parish is no longer the only way to organize Christians (the automobile has made nonsense of the old 'local' congregation anyway : we can all pick and choose within a wide radius of home). It is perhaps disappointing to a local minister if his young people go off to some exotic church or action group down town; but would he rather that they gave up Christian worship and service altogether? And sometimes that is the only likely alternative.

A third essential is that the whole institutional Church must recognize, in its organization and in its setting of priorities, that what 'world oriented' Christians do, be they young or old, in their daily work and study and service and leisure is *their proper vocation under Christ, and in no sense inferior or less important than 'church work'*. We repeat this point because it is really crucial. Unless politically minded and socially involved Christians are recognized as deeply committed members of the Body of Christ, then they will be increasingly alienated from the institutional churches.

And here we come to the heart of the matter. We can experiment with different styles of church worship and education. We can have special groups of Christian journalists, politicians, and so on. But in the last resort we have to make and to hold to painful decisions about staff and financial priorities. And we have to accept the hard fact: no army can be run for the sake of its head-quarters personnel or for its old-age pensioners. Nor can the 'army' of the Lord.

Of course, it can't be run for the sake of the young laity under twenty-five either. The Christian Church operates, and must be trained and supported, for the job of serving the Lord and his world. But church leader-ship and finance must be concentrated more on the 'front-line troops', more on the 'combat units', more on the specialist skills and endurance training and orienta-tion courses required by these people, and less on the relatively minor role to be played by the veterans of the past.

This will perhaps sound a little callous and harsh. It is not at all meant to be callous: the sharp note is neces-sary. Of course we should be courteous, considerate, patient (when we have time), and careful in our dealings with the established leaders and solid citizens of the churches. Of course they are worthy of respect for their faithful service in the past. Of course they may deserve the dignity and courtesy due to veterans. But the Church has a fighting job to do, and we are losing our active service men. Their needs and training must come first.

Many of the more conservative people in our churches know this at the back of their minds. Some of them resent the new emphasis on youth and change, but many of them are asking themselves uneasily: 'And what is going to happen in ten years, or in twenty, if we do not change things? Where is the leadership for the future?' It is one of the most painful and noble and necessary sacrifices in any human organization when veterans accept that their good ways of the past are not good ways for the future. The Church is not exempt from this process; and it is not right for church leaders to pretend otherwise.

In actual fact, when once this kind of problem is faced fairly and squarely in national or in local church life, once the principle is established that the people outside are what matters supremely, then it is often wonderful how graciously older or more conservative people accept this. Sometimes radicals greatly underestimate the sacrifices which more traditional church people will make if they see that these are really necessary for the work of God. But if senior church members are to turn bitter, if they are determined to be offended, then offended they must be. Their feelings—and yours and ours—are not more important than the urgent jobs to be done.

We have no desire to end this American edition of *God's Lively People* on an entirely sombre note. There is perhaps quite enough gloom and despondency in the churches of the United States at the present time. Indeed, we would dare to conclude with the thoroughly unfashionable assertion that there are still many signs of hope, many possibilities for the future, in the churches of the United States today. It cannot be at all easy for an American Christian who knows the frightening difference between the euphoric church growth of the 1950s and the doubts and arguments of today to realize how much strength, how much potential there still is in his country's churches and congregations. He is also much tempted to fall into the false and almost masochistic assumption that they are somehow bound to decline in numbers and in influence in the same way as has happened in Britain and northern Europe. They may; but this is surely not at all inevitable.

For one thing, American church life and growth have been quite different from the position in Europe for many years: it is superficial to assume that now the two patterns must conform. Certainly there are some common Western tendencies in urbanization, secularization, and in the development of leisure styles, but this is not to say that the American churches must be so unintelligent, so faithless, and so much captive to contemporary trends that they follow entirely the European example in church decline. Surely the famous doctrine of hope suggests that the future here, as elsewhere, is at least partially open.

We are also impressed by certain continuing strengths in the American denominations. They now report that they are increasingly short of dollars; but they are not poor in anything like the same way that many other churches in the world are. They are worried about a shortage of able clergy and other leaders but there are still thousands of competent and committed people in church work. They voice justifiable complaints about their conservative and pietistic and unresponsive laity; but there are still hundreds of sensible, lively and most promising lay people around. (Where would most of the radical and reforming movements inside and outside the 'system' be without the help of church people?) Some British and European commentators seem very ready (today as in the past) to write off the great American churches as declining giants: this is neither courteous nor intelligent.

But the pace of change outside accelerates. Great human institutions do decay today with alarming speed. We believe that our fellow Christians in North America still have a chance to renew their vision and to build up their laity for the future. But these matters are very urgent. The options will not be open for much longer.

Bibliography—
Books for Further Reading

Chapter 1—*A Commitment to the Future*

Kahn, H., and Wiener, A. J., *The Year 2000*. The Macmillan Company, 1967. A very important book, though not always easy reading.

U.S. Commission on the Year 2000. Interim Report in *Daedalus* special issue, October 1968.

Clarke, Arthur C., *Profiles of the Future*. Bantam Books, 1967.

Schultz, Hans Jürgen, *Conversion to the World*. London SCM Press, Ltd, 1967.

Gibbs, Mark, and Morton, T. Ralph, *God's Frozen People*. The Westminster Press, 1965.

Chapters 2 and 3

As promised in the text (p. 43) we give some special notes for these chapters. It is not necessary for lay men and women to study modern theological books in order to think theologically. It is more important that they should be thinking about the world and God in terms of their own experience. But it helps to know what the professional theologians are saying. At present there are some movements in theology which should be of great interest to the laity. Vital theological thinking is always a response to what is happening in the world. It helps us to understand our own situation and the relevance of the Christian faith to it.

Here it is impossible to do more than to suggest a few books of particular interest. These can be divided into three groups, though these groups overlap.

1. *Books which assert the essentially lay nature of the Church*

Kraemer, Hendrik, *A Theology of the Laity*. The Westminster Press, 1959. This is the pioneer book in this section.

Congar, Yves, *Priest and Layman*. London : Darton, Longman and

Todd, 1967. A Roman Catholic scholar's rather rambling reflections on the place of the laity.

Hoekendijk, J. C., *The Church Inside Out*. The Westminster Press, 1966.

Ayres, Francis O., *The Ministry of the Laity*. The Westminster Press, 1966. A most useful statement from a distinguished American experimenter in laity education.

Weber, Hans-Ruedi, the journal *Laity*, and other publications of the World Council of Churches, have included some very important articles from this European leader in laity education.

2. *Books which assert the essentially secular nature of Christianity*

These books assert the word 'secular' over against the word 'religious', as those in the last section asserted 'lay' over against 'clerical'. They argue that the Christian faith has to do with the secular world and does not offer a religious escape from it. This, of course, is no new idea. It is basic to the doctrines of Creation and Incarnation. In its more modern form it has found expression in such phrases as 'religionless Christianity' and 'holy worldliness'. Its prophets were the German theologians Bultmann, Tillich, and, especially, Bonhoeffer. Their works are too many to list here. In Britain there have been men like John MacMurray and Donald MacKinnon who have been making the same emphasis in different language.

The following contemporary books are useful:

Robinson, John A.T., *Honest to God*. The Westminster Press, 1963.

———— *The New Reformation?* The Westminster Press, 1965.

———— *On Being the Church in the World*. The Westminster Press, 1962.

———— *Exploration Into God*. Stamford University Press, 1967.

Leeuwen, A. Th. van, *Christianity in World History*. Charles Scribners Sons, 1966. This is the classical book on the secular nature of Christianity. It sees secularization as the clue to the purpose of history and the peculiar contribution of the Bible and of Christian doctrine. Its background is not Europe but the world. A difficult book but very important.

Gregor Smith, Ronald, *The Whole Man*. The Westminster Press, 1969.

———— *Secular Christianity*. London: William Collins Sons & Co., Ltd, 1966.

———— *The Doctrine of God*. The Westminster Press, 1970. A very important book.

Cox, Harvey, *The Secular City*. The Macmillan Company, 1965. The subtitle of this famous paperback indicates its scope 'Secularization and Urbanization in Theological Perspective'. The theological part is stimulating and readable; the sociological part is perhaps a bit less satisfying.

Buren, Paul M. van, *The Secular Meaning of the Gospel*. The Macmillan Company, 1963. This rather difficult book, which came out before *Honest to God*, is revolutionary in its discarding of many theological ideas while maintaining the centrality of Jesus.

Most of these books are prepared by theologians for theologians. As relevant and perhaps more important to lay people are the writings of John Wren-Lewis, who writes out of his experience in the scientific world. His articles are to be found in many magazines and papers, and he has also a chapter in *Faith, Fact and Fantasy*. The Westminster Press, 1966.

3. *The 'Death of God' Theology*

The name shocks many and puzzles most, but its more correct title of 'Radical Theology' conveys no meaning at all. We should not let this name blind us to its meaning or its importance. It arises directly out of our new secular society and can help us to understand it. Although its roots go back into European literature and philosophy, it is essentially an American movement of the '6os.

The two main writers of this school are William Hamilton and Thomas J. J. Altizer. The most convenient books to read are :

Altizer, Thomas J. J., and Hamilton, William, *Radical Theology and the Death of God*. Penguin Books, Inc., 1968.

Altizer, Thomas J. J., *The Gospel of Christian Atheism*. The Westminster Press, 1966.

They deny that they are teaching 'sheer atheist humanism'. Perhaps we should not be so shocked by the words 'death of God' if we remember how central to Christian thinking is the 'death of Jesus'. Certainly they are thinking in this context. The person of Jesus occupies a commanding, central position in their thought. They would claim that the phrase 'death of God' means more than that modern man has lost his sense of God or that our ways of talking about God mean nothing to us now. They claim that something has happened to the world and to men that has freed men from the idea, and indeed from the fact, of God. Altizer would say that we are now 'waiting in silence'. Hamilton is more willing to hint that he is waiting, not for a God we need, but for a God to enjoy.

Their thinking sheds a new light on the world and on ourselves.

The books in these three sections point to the possibility of
an open theology, which is the only kind of theology to which
lay people today can make a contribution.

Chapter 4—*Worship and the Laity*

Heuvel, Albert H. van den, *The Humiliation of the Church*.
The Westminster Press, 1966. Particularly Chs. 4 and 5.

Risk, Vol. 5, No. 1, 1969. 'Living: Liturgical Style'. Geneva:
World Council of Churches.

Bloy, Myron B., Jr, ed., *Multi-media Worship*. The Seabury Press,
Inc., 1969.

Many new ideas about new styles of worship are available
from The Associated Parishes, 116 West Washington Avenue,
Madison, Wisc. 53703, and (on church music) from The Shaw-
nee Press, Delaware Water Gap, Pa. 18327.

Chapter 5—*Prayer and the Laity*

The books that help us to pray are those that awaken us to
the fact that our own thoughts, worries, questions, and joys
are the material of prayer. Such books are rare and very
personal. There are the books of:

Quoist, Michel, *Prayers of Life*. Dublin: M. H. Gill & Sons, Ltd,
1963.

Boyd, Malcolm, *The Book of Days*. Random House, Inc., 1968.

Just as valuable are the Bible and modern poetry.

Chapter 6—*The Bible is for Adults*

We do not give a list of commentaries, partly because there
are so many of them and they are generally available, but
mainly because we doubt whether they are what lay people
need to help them to read the Bible. Of course some knowledge of how the book came to be written is necessary if only
to save us from any fundamentalist worship of the printed
word. Perhaps the greatest help is to have some knowledge of
general literature and some idea of how books come to be
written. The danger is to think that the Bible is a different

kind of book in the method of its production. It is also good to have some knowledge of the economic and political background.

But none of these different kinds of useful information helps us to see what the Bible, or any book of it, is all about. The books that can help are those which in some way awaken us to the situations people were and are in, and the questions that confront them. Here are some suggestions:

Smart, Ninian, *Secular Education and the Logic of Religion*. London: Faber & Faber, Ltd, 1968.

Christ for Us Today: Papers from the 50th Annual Conference of Modern Churchmen. London: SCM Press, Ltd, 1967.

Tennant, Roger, *Born of a Woman*. London: S.P.C.K., 1961.

Morton, T. Ralph, *The Twelve Together*. Glasgow: Iona Community, 1956.

Chapter 7—*What Has Gone Wrong?*

Besides the books mentioned above for Chapters 2 and 3, we suggest:

Congar, Yves, *Lay People in the Church*. Newman Press, 1957.

Bonhoeffer, Dietrich, *Letters and Papers from Prison*. The Macmillan Company, 1967.

Oldham, J. H., *Life Is Commitment*. Harper & Brothers, 1953. An abridged edition is available in the Association Press Reflection Books series, 1959.

Hunter, David R., *Christian Education as Engagement*. The Seabury Press, Inc., 1963.

Russell, Letty M., *Christian Education in Mission*. The Westminster Press, 1967. A valuable report of experiments from the East Harlem Protestant Parish.

Russell, Ken, and Tooke, Joan Doreen, *Learning to Give as Part of Religious Education*. Oxford: Pergamon Press, 1967.

Bergevin, Paul, Morris, Dwight, and Smith, Robert M., *Adult Education Procedures*. The Seabury Press, Inc., 1968.

Fry, John R., *A Hard Look at Adult Christian Education*. The Westminster Press, 1961.

Ramsay, William McDowell, *Cycles and Renewal Trends in Protestant Lay Education*. Abingdon Press, 1969. A summary of various trends in Protestant laity education over the last twenty years. Concise and informative.

Chapter 8—*Laity Education at the Local Level*

Casteel, John L. (ed.), *The Creative Role of Interpersonal Groups in the Church Today.* Association Press. 1968.

Kempes, Robert H., and Trefz, Edward K. (ed.), *Lay Education in the Parish.* The Geneva Press, 1968.

Morton, T. Ralph, *The Household of Faith.* Glasgow: Iona Community, 1951.

Chapters 9, 10, and 11

Centres of Renewal. Geneva: World Council of Churches, 1964. A popular introduction to many residential centres.

Frakes, Margaret. *Bridges to Understanding.* Muhlenberg Press, 1960. Still the best introduction to the lay academies in Europe, though a book on more recent developments is needed and is now in preparation.

Morton, T. Ralph, *The Iona Community Story.* London: Lutterworth Press, 1957.

Oldham, J. H., *Florence Allshorn and the Story of St Julian's.* Harper & Brothers, 1952. The famous no-fuss no programme centre in Sussex, England.

Chapter 12—*Large Public Events in Laity Education*

Littell, Franklin H., *The German Phoenix.* Doubleday & Company, Inc., 1960.

Hühne, Werner, and Mark Gibbs (ed.), *A Man to Be Reckoned With.* London: SCM Press, Ltd, 1961. The story of Thadden-Trieglaff and the German Kirchentag.

These are two good books with details about the earlier days of the Kirchentag. There is nothing yet in English on the movement since 1962, though a symposium is now being prepared.

Chapter 13—*The Education of Christian Revolutionaries*

Heuvel, Albert H. van den, *These Rebellious Powers.* Friendship Press, 1965. Essays on sex, money, nationalism, racism, and religion.

Klugmann, James, and Oestreicher, Paul, *What Kind of Revolution?* London: Panther Books, 1968. (N.B. for U.S. readers: This firm has nothing to do with the Black Panthers.)

Vincent, John, *The Race Race*. London: SCM Press, Ltd, 1970. A report on the World Council of Churches 1969 consultation on racism.

Morris, Colin M., *Unyoung, Uncolored, Unpoor*. Abingdon Press, 1969.

Oppenheimer, Martin, *The Urban Guerrilla*. Quadrangle Books, Inc., 1970. The practical difficulties of violent urban revolution.

Hessel, Dieter T., *Reconcilation and Conflict*. The Westminster Press, 1969. Church controversy over social involvement.

Oglesby, Carl, and Shaull, Richard, *Containment and Change*, The Macmillan Company, 1967.

Berger, Peter, and Neuhaus, Richard J., *Movement and Revolution*. Doubleday & Company, Inc., 1970. A 'conservative' and a 'radical' argue about the possibilities of violent revolution.

Brown, John Pairman, *The Liberated Zone*. John Knox Press, 1969.

────── *Planet on Strike*. The Seabury Press, Inc., 1970. Two extremely radical books from the theologian of the Free Church of Berkeley, California.

Ellul, Jacques, *Violence*. London: SCM Press, Ltd, 1970.

Chapter 14—*The Way Forward*

McBrien, Richard Peter, *Do We Need the Church?* Harper & Row, Publishers, Inc., 1969. A serious Roman Catholic work.

Morris, Colin M., *Include Me Out!* Abingdon Press, 1968. Violent anti-institutional church stuff, which is acceptable to more laity than we like to think.

Grubb, Sir Kenneth, *A Layman Looks at the Church*. London: Hodder & Stoughton, Ltd, 1954, 1964. A veteran and outspoken church layman gives some frank and lively comments.

Cox, Harvey, *God's Revolution and Man's Responsibility*. Judson Press, 1965.

Heuvel, Albert H. van den, *The Humiliation of the Church*. The Westminster Press, 1966. A major contribution on the work of young adult laity.

The Church for Others and the Church for the World. Geneva: World Council of Churches, 1967. The reports of the 'missionary structure of the congregation' studies.

Rose, Stephen C., 'The Grassroots Church,' *Renewal Magazine*, 1968.
—— (ed.), 'Who's Killing the Church?' *Renewal Magazine*, 1966.
Boyd, Malcolm (ed.), *The Underground Church*. Pelican Books, 1969. Some highly visible examples of informal and underground churches.